Year of Action

*How to Stop Waiting & Start Living
Your BIG, Fabulous Life*

ঙ

*Here's to your
Year of Action!*

Erin McCormick

Erin Moran McCormick

Year of Action: How to Stop Waiting & Start Living Your BIG,
Fabulous Life

By Erin Moran McCormick

Library of Congress Control Number: 2012950935
ISBN: 978-0-9853096-0-2
Published by: Year of Action, 5 Nye Road, Medfield, MA 02052
Printed in the United States of America
First printing October 2012

Book design: Erin Moran McCormick
Cover Illustration: Mellefrency/Shutterstock.com

Except where noted, all photos and illustrations courtesy of
Erin Moran McCormick

To contact the author for speaking engagements, press and other
inquiries:
Erin@YearofAction.com

For other information please visit:
www.YearofAction.com

Follow me: @YearofAction

For my parents,
Mary & Mickey Moran,
who always made me believe that I could do anything.

ʚɞ

TABLE OF CONTENTS

BUILD STRONG RELATIONSHIPS

GET LOST

GET FOUND

LIVE YOUR ONE WILD & PRECIOUS LIFE

*"Tell me, what is it you plan to do
with your one wild and precious life?"*
- MARY OLIVER

- Introduction -

I don't have a cape. Last time I checked I couldn't leap tall buildings either. But I am an *Action Hero*; and you can be too. Starting right now.

Just like mild-mannered Clark Kent or painfully shy Peter Parker, you can't always spot an *Action Hero*. They look like average, everyday people. (Although, c'mon – do you expect me to believe that Lois Lane *really* did not know that Clark was Superman?) That aside, you may not know that *you* have *Action Hero* possibility - but I'm here to tell you, YOU DO. It is yours for the taking and this book is here to help you learn how.

I should probably tell you that my definition of an *Action Hero* is a bit different than that of Marvel Comics™. For me, an *Action Hero* is someone who can turn seemingly little moments into the stuff of which great lives are made. My *Action Hero* is someone who uses these ordinary moments as momentum to take action and create extraordinary lives.

It is someone like you.

Being an *Action Hero* for my life has been an exhilarating way to live and something that I never thought I could do. At age 25, I undertook my first *Year of Action.* I went from being afraid of raising my hand in class or asking my boss for a day off, to quitting my job and following my dream - buying a one-way ticket to Europe. I travelled on my own, worked in Piccadilly Circus in London, touched Mozart's piano in Salzburg and saw my favorite work of art - Michelangelo's *Pietà* in Rome. I celebrated Christmas by a fireside in Ireland and made my personal dream come true, my *pièce de résistance,* I had an apartment in Paris overlooking the Eiffel Tower.

It's a journey that I never thought I could take - and it's a journey that I know you can take too - the journey towards finding what makes you happy and taking action to live the life you want.

I can hear you saying, "Well, it's one thing to do what you want when you are young and don't have a care in the world BUT it is quite another for me. I have a family. I have a mortgage. I need the health insurance. I don't have any savings. I don't have a fancy degree. I don't have anyone to help me. I can't even make ends meet. I am not that brave. I... *(insert really good excuse here)."*

Yet, before you dismiss this *Year of Action* way of living, telling yourself that YOU can't do what you want to because *(see really good excuses above)*, you should know that this year, on my 50th birthday, I set out upon my second *Year of Action.* I quit my job in the worst economy in recent history, without a new job in place. A.K.A. "Are you a &^*!@# idiot?" "Who quits their job in this economy?" "That's just how it is – just tough it out."

Really? Is that all there is?

The day I quit, one of my co-workers died suddenly. How long are you supposed to wait to enjoy your life - to be happy? Enough is enough. I believe there is more to life than just keeping your head down and "toughing it out." I deserve more...and so do you.

Fortunately, becoming an *Action Hero* for your life is not some special power with which you have to be born. You can *learn* how to do this. The first phase is learning to "see" the big and small moments. The second phase is believing in the possibility that these moments are showing you. And the third phase is taking a step - a small, tiny step...and then another one. You will gain momentum with each stride. Soon enough, what seemed impossible at first, starts to feel normal.

The *Year of Action* process:

1. See the moment.
2. Believe in the possibilities.
3. Take a step...and then another one.

Just because it is a simple process, do not underestimate its incredible power. Unfortunately, many people shut their eyes and ears to their life moments. So they never get started. *YOU* never get started. But I believe you can. And I believe you will. I invite you (dare you) to try this *Year of Action* way of living. You won't believe it!

In this book, I walk you through the moments that I took away from my two *Years of Action*. When I was 25 and traveled to Europe; and then at 50, when I quit my job to focus on some more personal goals like writing this book, losing weight and finding work I love.

It doesn't matter if you're 25, 50 or 75. Start somewhere. Start today. It just takes a *moment* to change and I am giving you that moment right now.

You have permission to start living your life.

This is not about being irresponsible or selfish. This is about conscious planning and choosing to live the life you want. There were times in my life when I wanted to quit my job but I didn't have my finances in order. That inspired me to get them in order so that I would have options and not be in that position again. It is about being brave *and* smart. (You wouldn't go skydiving without a parachute.)

We postpone our lives thinking we'll always have tomorrow. Thinking there will be time another day - another week - another year.

"I'll do it later." "I can't." "I'm busy." "Not now." "I could never do that anyway." "This is all there is."

I want to change that for you.

People write a lot about change - about changing your life. Yet, even if we *want* to do something, the *thought* of change is so hard. We get comfortable with our habits, even if they are not what make us happy. We get so used to the status quo that after a while, change seems too daunting, too tough and too impossible…so we don't.

Change is about the little things. About taking a little step… and then another one. It's about realizing that life is precious and you can't waste any time. It's about finding your why, your MOMENT and using that as your MOMENTUM to take action on your life.

What a way to make a living

Recently, I overheard my husband on the phone with a telemarketer who was painfully reading from a script. He listened patiently to the poor woman diligently reciting word for word in a monotone voice, before he finally said, "No thank you." I wondered why he didn't just hang up right away.

He said, "I feel bad for her. She probably gets phones slammed in her ear all day long. What a way to make a living."

How did she get there? How do any of us get where we are in life? Is this all there is? If you want to change, how do you get out from all of this? Where do you even start?

For my 25-year-old self, it started with a pile of posters rolled up on the floor near my bed in my first apartment. I had been stepping over them every day and it suddenly dawned on me that it had been MONTHS since I moved in to this apartment. MONTHS. And then a *moment* happened. I thought, "Is this how I am going to live? Am I going to go through life putting things off or am I going to do things and take action?"

My *Year of Action* was born.

Right then I decided that I would DO things and not step over or around them. I realized it doesn't take a fanfare and fireworks to change. It just takes a *moment*. Then it's all about how you make that moment last and infuse it in with your life.

My first *Year of Action* was so successful that it became more than just doing things that I had been putting off. I started forcing myself to act on things that I was afraid to do - things that took guts. (I would do a fist pump and say, *"Year of Action,"* when I started to make excuses for not acting and it helped give me strength and motivation.)

Motivation is key. That's why I have my YEAR *of Action* – which is more a state of mind than a physical date. Its motivation is from life's moments. These moments are what you can hold on to when you want to quit and revert back to your old ways.

So many New Year's resolutions fail because a random date (January 1st) isn't a strong motivator. There's no *moment* or meaning attached to it. When things get tough and you want to quit, thinking of January 1st won't help. Plus, moments can happen at *any* time and allow you to start taking action on *any* day – *like today!*

ᑳ

I am still shaking from the drive to the Emergency Room. Nurses and doctors scurry around me in a blur - yet amid all the chaos, my life suddenly became very clear. All my little worries didn't matter any more. I had thought my biggest news that day was going to be that I had quit my job. A decision that, as the family breadwinner, I had been debating - struggling - really agonizing over - for nearly two years. This was supposed to be a night to relax and celebrate.

Instead, my twelve-year-old had a severe allergic reaction to pine nuts and was rushed to the hospital. It is frightening how quickly it all happens and how fast things get put into perspective.

You never feel more aware of how precious life is than when you are in a hospital. Suddenly my big scary decision to quit a toxic work environment was simple and one of the smartest things I had done in a long time.

Most importantly, my son is fine.

It's funny that after laboring for so long over my decision to quit my job, in one *moment* in the hospital, I remembered that life is short and I didn't want to waste it in a job that made me so unhappy.

It brought me back to what I learned 25 years ago. Life is about *moments* - little tugs and whispers - that often happen when we're not even paying attention - moments that change your life forever. Whether you call it The Universe, God, inspiration, spirituality, gut instinct or luck - these moments are right in front of us, helping us find our way and giving us a roadmap to our lives - if we will just let them.

I filled six journals during my first *Year of Action* and started blogging a few years before my second *Year of Action*. This book has excerpts from these writings along with how I learned to "see the moments" in my life - ordinary moments that lead to small steps which brought big changes; turning ordinary into extraordinary.

Each chapter focuses on a *moment* accompanied by examples and *Action Steps* that you can take in your life. Taking action can be anything: cleaning out the clutter in your house, losing weight, quitting a toxic job, hopping a plane to Paris or following a dream. I know because I've done all of these. I never thought I could, but I did. I want to show you how I did it and help you do it too.

Usually small steps are all you need. But every once in a while, you may need to take a big step – you may need to leap – like I did at age 25 and then again at age 50. (Who knows what I'll do at 75?) This book has moments from both of these *Year of Action* "leap years" as well as the important small action steps that lead you to the big changes.

My hope is that my everyday adventures (the good, the bad and the embarrassing), practical advice and lessons learned will help to transform YOU into an *Action Hero* for your life – to inspire you to create the life you were meant to live. Remember, you hold the power to take action to create your BIG, fabulous life. It starts right now. *Year of Action!*

Turn moments
into action

∛

Chapter 1

See the moments.

"Life isn't a matter of milestones, but of moments."
– ROSE FITZGERALD KENNEDY

This section is a collection of how I learned to start "seeing my moments" which I then used as the momentum to create my first Year of Action.

Paris, May 1986

I am holding on for dear life. We just went down a hill into a tunnel and the roar of the engine is so loud echoing off the walls. I'm glad that I don't know how to translate *km* into *mph* because I don't really want to know how fast we're going.

I am on the back of a motorcycle in Paris with a French racecar driver – who takes my breath away – and I smile and think to myself, "How did I get here?"

People Express - a $99, one-way ticket to Belgium, to be exact. (It was the cheapest place they flew.)

Well that, plus a year of thinking and a lifetime of dreaming about doing this. Still, it's hard to believe it was actually happening.

The toughest part is believing that you can do it. Many people say things like, *"I have always wanted to… learn to play the piano, go to Hawaii, start my own business, write a book"* – yet it never gets past that.

You talk yourself into believing that YOU could never do something like that. Especially when there are a number of forces working against you.

Author and marketing guru Seth Godin calls it the lizard brain[1], the voice in the back of your head telling you that you can't.

There's always a good reason NOT to do something. For me, my lizard brain was in full force telling me I couldn't go. I didn't speak French. I didn't know anyone in France. I didn't have a place to stay. I didn't have a work visa. I didn't have much money. The friend I was planning to travel with couldn't go at the last minute.

So how *did* I get here?

The year leading up to my decision had been tough. I knew it was time to leave my job. I had been working non-stop for weeks – including weekends – on a huge project. A turning point was when one of the executives sought me out to come work for him. It was a promotion and a big job in his department. We discussed the terms, the transition and I accepted.

He came back the next day and said that he had never offered me a job and besides, what made me think I could do that job anyway?

It played right into my lizard brain. My instinct was to just skulk away thinking, "Yeah he's right." But I didn't walk away. *Year of Action!* I spoke up for myself. I pointed my finger at him and said, "I don't know what happened between yesterday and today but you and I both know that you offered me the job." I left the building and walked home. (Remember - always get it in writing!)

I found out later that my boss didn't want to lose me and told the man who made me the offer to go back and tell me that I wasn't good enough for the job. I ended up moving to a different department but I knew that this company wasn't where I wanted to stay.

But even more than work woes, my heart was broken. The three key people in my life (my roommate; my first love who was back in my life; and a dear friend from work – whom I spent all my time with) were all getting married that year.

As happy as I was for them, I was devastated. Not only would I have to move, these people were my life. I poured so much of my energy into each of these relationships only to have them all move on without me.

What was I doing?

My lizard brain would have had me stay put at the company and feel sorry for myself. Luckily, I didn't listen.

Setting the stage

I never raised my hand in high school. In fact, I don't remember saying much of anything in class. I worked hard and had a nice group of friends, but I was afraid to speak up; afraid to go out on the limb.

You should know that I won the "family lottery." I was born into an incredible family and had a great childhood. We laughed with (and fought and teased) each other. But we were there for each other. We didn't have a lot of money but we didn't know it.

My mother would often say, "We are proud of you and all your accomplishments," which would unleash sibling mocking and teasing. But deep down hearing that, set the stage for us to believe in ourselves. My parents made us feel that we could do anything. This is an incredible gift. They set great examples and instilled in us many positive beliefs, which laid the groundwork for a wonderful life.

A major *moment* in my life happened in high school. When I was 16, my father had a heart attack and was given his last rites on the night of my brother's high school graduation. I had never really been in a hospital before. He didn't let my younger siblings into the Intensive Care Unit but he had me come in.

It was just the two of us in that big, open white room and he had tears in his eyes. It was the first time I had ever seen him cry. We said our goodbyes. It was eerily quiet.

I don't remember much more than that. But I have replayed that scene in my mind - walking into that room and seeing him laying there - hundreds, perhaps thousands, of times.

Then it was incredible. He lived! Something inside me changed. I didn't know it then - but it did. A *moment:*

Life, as you know it, can change in an instant.
You can't take anything for granted.

One Sunday, after church, my mother and I bumped into the Greenes. Their daughter was a freshman (or as they say now *first year*) at Smith College. I had never heard of Smith. When I found out it was "all girls" (or as I say now, *all women*) I thought, "No way!"

My parents convinced me to take a look. (My father was motivated by the amount of money they gave in scholarships.) We arranged for a weekend visit with Maura Greene. I reluctantly agreed. I had never been away from home. I'll just do this and get them off my back. I would **NEVER** go to an "all girls" school.

I loved it.

I walked into the art building, the art studios, the museum and I was hooked. This place was magnificent. I had an unbelievable weekend. There were parties and fun and it was nothing like I had imagined. The young women were fabulous. Nice. Welcoming. Smart. Funny. And there were tons of guys on campus. Seems the whole "all girls" thing is actually a big draw!

I applied. When I came back to campus for my interview, as I was turning the handle to the door of the Admissions Office I turned back to ask my mother, "What am I supposed to say anyway?"

She said, "Just be yourself."

Just be yourself.

No coaching. No SAT prep courses. No elaborate tutors about interview skills. I just was myself. I got in. Early Decision. I also got an amazing scholarship. A huge *moment:* December 15, 1978 – getting accepted to Smith.

Never say never.

Smith College

Smith was a life changing experience for me. I grew up in Worcester, Massachusetts, about an hour outside of Boston. My parents were teachers. Most of my friends were like me from middle class, Irish, Catholic families. Suddenly I was living with wealthy women from around the world. On my hall were women from Sri Lanka, Beverly Hills and Colombia to name a few. I had never been away from home. I didn't have a passport. No trust fund. I didn't know which fork to use.

My first semester, I took a course with the dean of the college. I waited until the last minute to get one of the books and it was sold out. I had to write a paper on this book so I tried to wing it.

I got a D. My first paper...a D? They made a mistake by accepting me. What was I doing here? How did I get in? I can't do it. I don't belong here. I got a D! How will I tell my parents when I flunk out?

The dean gave me a second chance. It was a Thursday and she said that I could have the weekend to rewrite it. I got the book, furiously read it over the weekend and rewrote the paper. It was a rainy Monday and I rode my bike over to College Hall. I remember sitting by myself at the biggest conference table I had even seen, waiting for the dean to come in. When she did, she made me feel at ease and sat down next to me. She saw that I had my new version in front of me and instead of looking at the paper, she just said to me, "Tell me about it."

We talked for about 40 minutes. She said, "Thank you" and took the paper. I headed back to my dorm. All week long I was nervous that I would flunk out of school. I got my paper back on Thursday. This time, I got an A. Another *moment*:

You do belong here. But guess what, *Einstein,*
you have to actually *do* the work!

It was at Smith that I really fell in love with art.

Another big moment, albeit seemingly small at the time, was a simple art assignment my freshman year. As a fluke, a prestigious, high-ranking professor taught my Design 101 class. One of our first assignments was to create a logo of our initials. Unlike my first paper for the dean, I spent a lot of time on this assignment and ended up using negative space to create the letters EM.

It was after this one *little* assignment that Professor Offner asked me if I wanted to be his apprentice in his studio.

Give it your all – even on the little things.

Besides getting me out of washing dishes – which was my campus job with my scholarship – Professor Elliot Offner had a huge impact on my life. He was an amazing artist, scholar and man. I worked for him my entire time at Smith. He was my art professor, advisor and mentor. Of the many things he taught me, a couple really stand out.

Each week we had to hang our work on the wall and the class would critique each other's art. It was painful at first. It was hard to hear, hard to not take it personally and hard to not argue or make excuses. After a few weeks of this, I realized that I was literally separate from my work. If someone didn't like my art, that wasn't me they were criticizing, it was my work – over there on the wall. Not me. I actually learned to embrace what others were saying and it helped my work improve.

You are not your work.

There was a sign hanging in the art studio that said, *"Have you stepped back from your painting lately?"* In art, when you are too close to something, you can't see it clearly.

Pointillism is where lots of dots of color combine to form images. It is only when you take a step back that it comes into focus.

In life, this happens all the time. You need to take a step back; to look at things from another perspective. Things become clear when you step away.

To have had such one-on-one teaching from a world-renowned artist is priceless, but more than that, my life is profoundly different for having had him in it.

I am thankful for the world of art he introduced me to, for unleashing the artist in me, for believing in me – having him pluck me out of all the amazing art students at Smith to be his apprentice – and for instilling in me a love and desire to have art in my life and to see all the art that I was learning about – up close and in person.

My dream started.

Have you stepped back from your painting lately?

At Smith, I was surrounded by people who spoke many languages, who travelled and experienced amazing things. I wanted to open up my world to these things too, but it was more than I dreamed possible.

One of my dearest friends at Smith was Heather. She and I met during her junior year while she was on an exchange semester from Bowdoin College. She was only at Smith for one semester but we became fast friends. She spent her second semester in France. *Hmmm.*

She is doing it. I still didn't think it was something that I could do. But the seed was planted.

I knew that I wanted to experience the magnificent works that I had only seen in books (and covering the walls in the *Hillyer* Art Building for the Art 100 final exam). I also wanted to be someone who, when random French passages popped up unexpectedly in books, would know what they meant. *Mais oui bien sur.*

I also was beginning to realize that as much as the work is important – it's really about the people. The relationships. The experience. I found a balance between the work and the relationships/experience. (Although some might say I leaned *too strongly* towards the relationships/experience side!) It's true that I didn't spend all my time in Neilson Library but I did spend it wisely. I spent it around the dinner table.

At Smith, you eat in beautiful dining rooms in your dorm. It's one of the best parts of Smith – well the food yes, but I meant the women. That's the real education.

We made a rule early on that you couldn't talk at the table about how much work you had. Because guess what, *everyone* has a huge workload. We talked about life and took deep breaths and laughed. Thanks to our beloved Blanche, the kitchen maven who let us linger long after the dining room had cleared and kept the coffee brewing. Kathie, Nancy, Diane, Isa, Anne, Poole, Leslie, Lois, Marie, Nora, Moe and Heather and the other fabulous women of Comstock House and "the Quad" are among my dearest friends, 25 years later. Friends, especially your women friends, are an amazing gift and are not to be taken for granted.

I had a great role model for this - my mother.

When I was growing up, every other Wednesday was *Bridge Night* – which meant that we couldn't use the good towels in the bathroom or eat any of the fancy dessert. That was for the Bridge Club. We would all be rushed upstairs and put to bed early and warned that basically, unless someone was bleeding, we were not to come down. I have great memories of falling asleep to raucous laughter from the dining room.

I didn't think much of it until one Wednesday night when I was home from college and the Bridge Club was at our house. I was no longer shooed upstairs. I was allowed to stay downstairs – albeit quietly and out of the way – and from the kitchen I could overhear the conversation.

It hit me that Bridge Night had nothing to do with playing cards. This was *Therapy* – a precursor to Girls Weekends and Girls Night Out. Incredible mothers who put families first. This was typically the only thing that they did for themselves. It was a few hours, every other Wednesday, where they could let their hair down and talk about family issues, concerns, fears – anything really – in a safe, trusting environment. There was unconditional support and lots of laughter (and great desserts).

These women have been there to celebrate the big moments and have stood by us during tough times. This doesn't just magically happen. You have to work at it. My mother has an amazing circle of friends and is a great friend to so many. It will be your relationships that matter in your life. Cherish and nourish them.

I would be remiss if I also didn't mention *The Pearls,* Worcester's own *Red Hat Society* type women – of which my mother is one. They are out of their minds – in a good way. They wear crazy clothes, sing, dance and truly embrace life. They are definitely *Action Heroes.*

Find and nurture deep relationships.

Another *moment* from Smith was from one of our beloved alumnae, Anne Morrow Lindbergh, Class of 1928. She gave a speech at Smith in 1978 entitled, *"The Journey Not the Arrival".*[2] This has been a powerful message in my life - learning to embrace the journey. It is also etched in my brain because it was one of the essay questions on the Smith application!

The journey, not the arrival, matters.

An art major? What are you going to do with that?

It was a pretty big deal that I was at Smith. My relatives came here with very little. My grandmother was only 18 when she got on a boat by herself from Ireland to come to the United States. She came with a single trunk that held all her possessions.

When I was 18, my mother gave me that trunk to take with me to Smith.

I was the first person in my family to leave Worcester and go away to school. It was an especially big deal that I got a scholarship, because I would never have been able to go to Smith otherwise.

So, when I told my parents that I was going to major in art and psychology, it didn't go over very well. My father thought it was a waste of all this hard work only to be without a job when I graduated. He was afraid of the whole "starving artist" thing.

He begged me to study something practical - like economics. So I did. It came easily to me - but I hated it. I took one more semester of it and that was that. I figured it wouldn't do me any good to study this, only to then take a job doing what I don't like - even if I did get A's.

Find what you love.
You can figure out later how to make it work.

The summer after my junior year, I got an internship at Houghton-Mifflin Publishing in Boston in the College Art Division. I loved it. It didn't pay anything (as in nothing) so I was also waitressing and picking up money as a temp wherever I could.

One of the jobs I had was giving out samples at a supermarket. I gave out Superman Peanut Butter. I had to say, "Superman Peanut Butter - the peanut butter you can look up to!" Really. I had to say that! I can't keep a straight face now just thinking about it. (So perhaps THIS was how my Action Hero training *really* started.)

I also gave out water before anyone had bottled water. People would laugh at me and say, "Water? You're selling water? Who would ever buy water when you can get it for free?"

I didn't care though because it allowed me to work in Boston and try out publishing.

> Know that some things are just a means to an end –
> do what you need to do.

At the end of the summer, the creative director at Houghton-Mifflin offered me a job when I graduated. I was thrilled. I was all set. I had a great senior year and moved to Boston after graduation.

There was one small hitch. The creative director was creating a special job for me. She left the company. When she left, so did my job. When I arrived, the new director said, "You can do some freelance work for us." I couldn't do freelance work. I had so little experience and I had no idea what I was doing. I had to find something else.

September 1983

Boston

I didn't know how it all worked with renting an apartment. Our rent was $900 a month ($300 each). I knew we needed first and last month's rent. So, with $700 in my pocket I got on a bus to Boston and figured I would be fine. It would be tight, but I could start "temping" and be all set. I had never heard about a security deposit - which is an additional month's rent. My brother Mike loaned me the difference, but now I was stuck.

I had no money, no job and no Plan B. While I was looking for full-time work, I needed to make some money quickly so I went to a temp agency.

My first job as a college graduate was at a leasing company at Post Office Square in downtown Boston. They put me in a room with no windows, with no other people and closed the door and had me sit there all day typing numbers on leases. It was like a giant jail cell.

They didn't show me where anything was or introduce me to anyone. They called me "the temp." As in, "What's 'the temp' doing?"

"Who's that?"

"That's 'the temp'."

Plus, I didn't know there was a *back button* on the typewriter to erase your mistakes and I couldn't get the numbers to line up correctly so I kept ripping out the leases and starting over. (This from someone who would later be a CIO and lead an innovation and technology group - but - I'm getting ahead of myself.)

I didn't last there long. (Thank goodness.)

It made an impact on me though. It taught me how NOT to treat people. I learned not to take people for granted or make assumptions about them. Everyone has talents - sometimes you have to just dig a little. I mean, here I was a college graduate – from Smith! I was jam-packed with talent - somewhere in there - if someone would have just taken a *moment* to look. I'm not just "the temp," and others aren't either.

> Treat everyone you meet with respect.
>
> Encourage them to astound you.

The agency called and asked if I could run a switchboard. I said, "I don't know. Is it hard?"

They said, "We'll call you back." They called back and said, "Forget the switchboard. We're going to send you to a new company that needs a lot of help." Another *moment*.

The next day I showed up at Spinnaker Software. It was a startup in Cambridge and we were all huddled in basement offices in Kendall Square. My first day at Spinnaker, I had just enough money to buy some chips and soda for lunch (health nut!) and still have enough to take the T home. I didn't realize until later in the day that I was given the wrong change and now I didn't have enough to ride the subway.

I didn't know anyone in Boston. I didn't know how to walk home. I didn't know what I was going to do. I hadn't spoken to anyone all day. There was one person in the office that I had met in the morning when I checked in. So, nearing the end of the day I went up to her out of the blue and said, "Hello. Um...would you like to buy some stamps?"

She was taken aback but said okay and gave me .40 for a couple of stamps. I could now make it home and borrow a few dollars from my roommates until payday. (This stamp purchaser and I became good friends and still get a good laugh over this.)

Use what you have – even if it's just two stamps.

I was hired at Spinnaker after a month of temping when the woman who hired me, quit. She had me planning a big trade show, CES – the Consumer Electronics Show - in Las Vegas and when she left no one else knew what was going on with CES so they hired me.

I had my first title (other than 'the temp'), Sales Communications. I had no idea what that meant but I was doing graphic design (the old-fashioned way with x-acto knives, spray mount and T-squares).

I loved Spinnaker. I lived at Spinnaker. It was an early '80s typical startup, lots of twenty-somethings running around, lots of coffee and snacks and jeans. A group of very funny, talented, super bright people working their butts off. It was a software company and I had never touched a computer.

I was thrown into the deep-end when we got a million dollar order to create a line of computer games for Walden Books *(Treasure Island, The Wizard of Oz, Nine Princes of Amber* and more) within an insanely short period of time. We didn't have enough people to do the work and didn't have time to find them. Another *moment*.

I knew design, but nothing about computers. Our VP of Engineering, a wizard from MIT, knew computers but not design. We were joined at the hip. I got the best, hands-on computer education anyone could ask for.

Spinnaker bought two *Via Video* computers, state-of-the-art at the time, which cost about $100,000 each and took up a whole room. You could create graphics once and save them to be automatically formatted for IBM PC, Apple IIe and Commodore 64 machines all at once. It was big stuff back then.

We worked non-stop. Our motto became, *"They said it couldn't be done."* A cab picked me up at 5 a.m. (before the T started running) so that we could work on the Via Video computers 24 hours a day. We ate, slept and lived there. We made our deadline.

With enough beer, pizza, talent and humor you can do pretty much anything - even the impossible.

It was an amazing time. Some of my best friends today are my Spinnaker friends. I learned that you *can* do the impossible. I learned about the magic of great teams all pulling in the same direction on a mission. And I learned what it was like to get burned out.

Calling in *well*

It was during this craziness that Marie, a dear friend from Smith, came to visit. It was October and I told her that I hadn't had a day off - even for my birthday - since August. 40+ days. Crazy hours. No break.

She said, "I'm kidnapping you" and we went to Martha's Vineyard.

It was fantastic. We rode bikes, had delicious meals and enjoyed the beautiful fall Saturday. When we looked at the ferry schedule for Sunday, it meant leaving early in the morning - just as I was starting to relax - to get back to the nutty fray. My boss had told me that I couldn't come in late on Monday. Just then a *moment* happened.

What was I doing? I haven't had a weekend off in weeks? If I'm that important and they can't function without me, then I am certainly not being paid enough. No. I am not going to live like this any longer. I'm staying.

On Monday morning, I calmly called in to work from the Vineyard. I told my boss, "I'm not calling in sick, I'm calling in *well*. I'm *well* enough to know that I need a day off. I'll be in tomorrow."

My eyes were opened. I have control over my own life. I'm young. I don't have a family to support. I don't have to stay. I fully expected to be fired the next day. And that was okay.

When I got back to work, there were stock options on my chair.

People will keep taking from you if you let them. It's up to you to stand up for yourself.

Music & marriage

Heather (from Smith) and Linda (LJ) were roommates at Bowdoin College and were moving to Boston. Their third roommate, Tasha, was "discovered" as a model while getting her Ph.D. at Boston University and moved to Europe. I took her spot and moved in with Heather and LJ after I graduated. It was a crazy time.

The morning we were moving into our apartment, LJ and I were sitting at an IHOP having coffee and thinking about the year ahead. LJ was working at a local record store and that morning as we were about to start a new year in a new apartment, she declared that she was going to meet Peter Wolf and work for CBS Records.

Dream big and be specific.

To follow her dream, LJ immersed herself in the music world. She started by working at Discount Records in Harvard Square. She knew everything about music. Every album. Latest bands. She knew what she loved and what she wanted. She became manager of a band, *The Trademarks*. LJ, Heather and I spent many nights at *Bunratty's* in Brighton and *The Rat* in Kenmore Square with Trademarks' Johnny Smoke, Rico Hollywood, Sonny Malone and Brock.

I'd get random calls, "Meet me at *Jason's* (later to be the *Hard Rock Cafe*). We're having dinner with David Hasselhoff" after he launched his new, yet *painful* album, *Night Rocker*.

I would answer the phone and it might be Maurice Starr, who

produced the *New Kids on the Block* or Peter Wolf. Yes, not only did LJ meet the ex - Mr. Faye Dunaway, he invited her to his recording studio on Newbury Street during the making of his *Lights Out* album.

Or I'd get a call to meet at a dive bar after work to hear some new bands. Since I came straight from work and was dressed up in 1980s suits, LJ told people I was "A&R." (A&R, I learned, was Artists and Repertoire - the people who find new talent.) I have never been so popular. People were buying me drinks, testing out band names and asking my advice.

LJ and I played on stage with *The Trademarks* at the *Inn Square Men's Bar* in Somerville. I played the tambourine. (I'm a pianist but the tambourine was about all I could muster on stage.) The next morning my hand was black and blue from slamming the tambourine so hard. It was my first night in a rock band. It was fantastic!

I learned a lot from living with LJ. She lived life to the fullest. She knew what she wanted and went after it. She wasn't afraid to try new things. She was spontaneous. She was a riot. She had guts. And, she was great to drag me along with her for the ride.

Meanwhile, Heather was getting serious with her boyfriend, Bill. Let me back up. Heather had been dating someone I'll call Tim, who was very handsome and going to be a doctor. But he was, how shall I put this...a jerk.

Heather was going to be starting a "real job" in the fall and had applied to waitress for the summer at Faneuil Hall at a place called, *Seaside*. She got the job. A *moment* that would change her life.

The night she got the job, she and I decided to go celebrate at *Seaside* and see what it was like. We were having a ball. It was the end of the night and we were just about to leave when we bumped into two guys. We weren't there to meet guys. Really. There were certainly other nights when we wanted to meet guys - but not that night. We truly were there just to laugh and celebrate.

These guys were funny and nice. One of them really seemed to like Heather. As we left to catch our train, we stopped in the Ladies Room. I said, "Heather, that guy seems great. We can't just walk out of here. You need to go give him your number." She didn't want to. I convinced her that we should just go back and see if they were still there. As we got close, I gave her a shove so she would land right in front of him and be forced to talk to him. She gave him her number.

This was Bill...her future husband.

Love shows up when you least expect it.

I loved Bill. First, because he knocked Tim out of the picture, and, second, because he was just a great, fun guy. He also had some great friends. We all spent a lot of time together and Heather and Bill got serious pretty quickly.

Heather and I were like sisters. We could tell each other anything. We had so many inside jokes and funny stories. I would call her while out on a date for moral support or to get advice. If one of us made a dish for a dinner party, the other one would take huge spoonfuls of it and rave about how good it was in a very loud voice - while discreetly throwing it away. (Neither of us could cook.)

We all had a ton of fun living together and life was good.

Plan B

It wasn't long before CBS offered LJ a big job in NYC and Heather got engaged. All of a sudden, life as I knew it was ending. They were moving on with their lives. What was I doing?

I was working crazy hours at Spinnaker.

And as Heather and LJ were busy with their lives, I had become very close with someone at work, Peter. Peter would pick me up in the morning and drive me to work. We would go out for lunch nearly every day and out to dinner at least three nights a week. He was one of the nicest, smartest people I had ever met and I loved being with him. We would talk for hours.

One night, we were out and I was trying my first martini when he made a toast, "Here's to me and my bride-to-be... Wendy." What? Who's Wendy? My heart sank.

"Waiter, another martini!"

Meanwhile, my first love, Rick, had come back into my life. He had a serious girlfriend but he was back in the area and started calling me. It would be long periods of time between calls and yet as soon as I would hear his voice, my heart would skip a beat. I hated that.

So, 1985 - Heather, Peter and Rick all were getting married.

I was burned out. My roommates were moving out. I loved people who were off-limits.

Now what?

"Kidnapper Marie" who had earlier spirited me away to Martha's Vineyard to take a break from my crazy work schedule, was planning on moving to London for work. She said, "Why don't you come with me?" *Hmmm.*

Yes - this is perfect. We'll go have our own adventure. I started making plans.

Then I got a call. Her plans changed. Her move was being postponed indefinitely. She wasn't going.

The Loud Family

After the whole, Peter/Wendy thing, I started hanging out with other people at Spinnaker - "The Loud Family", to be specific - a funny, smart, boisterous gang that loved to laugh and have fun. We had potluck dinners where dessert was JELL-O™ with Twinkies™ floating in it. They did things like drive all night to L.L. Bean™ in Maine to buy orange hunting hats and ate circus peanuts. Three of the guys had been talking about taking a trip to Europe.

When they heard my friend couldn't go, they said, "Why don't you come with us?"

"Mom, Dad, umm... you know how I was going to go to London with Marie? Well... now, I'm buying a one-way ticket to Brussels with three guys."

I tried to make the case that it would be a lot safer to go with others than go by myself. And besides they are good guys.

It didn't go over well.

I come from a family of worriers. You wouldn't know this from the outside looking in, but it's true. Especially my Dad. He was always worrying.

My father was the sixth of seven children. His father died, after a long battle with cancer, when my dad was in high school. My dad never had a new bike or new clothes. Money was always a concern. You ate quickly because you didn't know if the food would run out before you had enough. (You certainly didn't quit a job and travel.)

So you can imagine how he felt about my plan.

I understood his concerns. After all, I am just like my Dad. I worry about everything. I spend a lot of energy trying not to worry, but it's in my nature. It's part of who I am but I have learned how to adapt. I remember my fourth grade teacher had me stand up so she could tell me, in front of the whole class, that I was going to have an ulcer by the time I was 21. (Nice, eh?) And BTW, [Miss R.,] I didn't!

So I know first-hand how hard change is. How hard action is when it's suppressed by all the worrying over what can go wrong. Yet after seeing my Dad in the hospital back in high school, I realized that you never really know what is going to happen and you certainly can't control it. You can make elaborate plans but life can change in a *moment*. If you want to do something, you need to do it now. And it's always good to have a Plan B.

It's always good to have a Plan B.

Have some fun!

A theme in my life started with a *moment* with my brother Jim. He had come to visit me at Smith College. He wanted me to do something. I forget the specifics (walk like a crab on the president's lawn, paint my face blue, howl like a coyote - you know normal stuff), but I said, "No. I can't do that – not at Smith."

He laughed and said, "Oh... is *that* how it's going to be? You're no fun anymore."

That was it.

From then on, whenever he wanted me to do something, he just said, "You're no fun anymore," and I would do it. (And I learned to start saying it to myself too.)

This can be a dangerous *moment* – so use it wisely. But it has served me well. From sneaking in with him to the 1986 Red Sox World Series, parasailing off a boat in Catalina, surfing (or more accurately *falling)* in huge waves at Huntington Beach, snorkeling with sharks, to crazy travel antics. It is a great reminder that life is short and you shouldn't take yourself too seriously. You need to laugh and have fun. Consider yourself warned with this one – and use it often!

You're no fun anymore!

I'm positive

People tell me that I'm lucky. People also tell me that I'm always smiling. I would have to agree on both counts. I am truly blessed and am so grateful for all that I have in my life.

This is not to say that I am always happy or that I live a charmed life – but rather I choose to live a life with a positive attitude. I believe that you get back or attract what you put out into the world and that you can make your own luck.

You get back what you give.

If you give out positive energy and have an attitude of giving, positive energy and giving will come back to you - in droves. You get back so much more than you give. So much so, that you never have to worry about it. If you just keep giving, it finds its way back to you. The inverse is also true. If you focus on the negative and complaining and being hurtful, that will also come back to you.

You get back what you give.
Be the most positive and giving person you know.

One of the reasons that I took the time to set the stage is to show you that I am probably a lot like you. I never thought I could do some of the things that I have done. I don't come from money. I went to public school. I worked very hard in school but I didn't have a lot of self-confidence. I worry a lot. Hell, I started out with two stamps to my name after college.

But after some of these *moments* - seemingly little moments - I started to pay attention. I started to incorporate them into my life.

The Moments

1. Life, as you know it, can change in an instant. You can't take anything for granted.

2. Just be yourself.

3. Never say never.

4. You do belong here - but you have to actually *do* the work!

5. Give it your all – even on the little things.

6. You are not your work.

7. Have you stepped back from your painting lately?

8. Find and nurture deep relationships.

9. The journey, not the arrival, matters.

10. Find what you love. You can figure out later how to make it work.

11. Some things are just a means to an end - do what you need to do.

12. Treat everyone you meet with respect. Encourage them to astound you.

13. Use what you have - even if it's only two stamps.

14. With enough beer, pizza, talent and humor you can do pretty much anything - even the impossible.

15. People will keep taking from you if you let them. It's up to you to stand up for yourself.

16. Dream big and be specific.

17. Love shows up when you least expect it.

18. It's always good to have a Plan B.

19. You're no fun anymore!

20. You get back what you give. Be the most positive and giving person you know.

As I read through this list of moments, I realize they are not just *my* moments. Although their context is unique to me, they are universal - moments that we all can use. They can also help jumpstart thinking about *your* moments.

Moments are a great roadmap for your life. They can fuel your courage to go from *thinking* about your life to actually *living* it - from tripping over posters of Paris to actually being there. Once you learn to start seeing the moments, it can help you build momentum to take a step and then another.

Once you start paying attention, you will be astounded at how often they show up. Leading the way. I now get goose bumps when I am on to something - when I am going in the right direction.

This book is a journey of how I put these *moments* into action – and how you can learn to do the same. You don't have to know what to do with *moments* – it is just important that you start to see them. Feel the tug. Take a step back and observe your life from a new perspective. Start asking what these moments are trying to tell you.

These moments are wake-up calls. Big and small "Aha" moments when you finally see something - when you acknowledge the tug that has been pulling at you.

WHAT are you doing? WHY are you doing this? What do you REALLY want? What's STOPPING you? What are you WAITING for?

Then it is about doing something. Anything. Taking a step. Often they are little steps. A dream said out loud. A decision to *not* live like this anymore. A last straw. All it takes is a *moment* to decide you want to change. You want something else. Something better. Something more. Then with each little step you take, you are building momentum that changes your life.

I have used these moments for the momentum to follow my dreams and to find work I enjoy, to find love and to create a better self. You can too.

See the moment

Talk ain't action - but it *is* cheap. It is easy to file away dreams or keep them vague: *"I want to travel - someday."* You *CAN* follow your dreams but it is all about taking action and it is hard to take action when the dream itself is vague. I had to believe that I could dream big. That it was *really* possible. It often starts with the moment, *"Have you stepped back from your painting lately?"* Take a look around your life.

WHAT are you doing?

Here's what I was doing before I went to Paris: *I'm working at a job I don't enjoy. I'm watching others get on with their lives. I'm burned out. I'm not happy but I need the money. I'm working crazy hours - for what? I feel a tug to leave but I'm stuck.*

 **ACTION STEP**: Now it's your turn. Take a step back and take a look at your life. Ask yourself WHAT are you doing with your life? Work? Relationships? Health? Fun? Write it down quickly and honestly – without any filters.

What does your life look like now? Write quickly and honestly:

_____

_____

_____

_____

_____

_____

_____

_____

_____

_____

_____

_____

WHY are you doing this?

I don't know. I haven't thought about why. I landed here after college and just started working hard. I am not finding joy here anymore but I don't know what to do or how to change. I just get up and go in to work without really thinking about why.

 **ACTION STEP**: Write down WHY you are doing what you are doing. Is it a means to an end? Do you have a plan? Is it just because you landed here and don't know what else to do? Does it bring you joy - *directly or indirectly?*

WHY are you doing what you're doing?

_____

_____

_____

_____

_____

_____

_____

_____

_____

_____

_____

What do you REALLY want?

I would love an adventure. I would like to shake things up a bit. I am young. I am not tied down. Instead of feeling badly about not being married like a lot of my friends, I can use it as a positive. I can do whatever I want. I could go to Paris! I could see all the art that I studied. I could learn to speak French. I could be one of those people who does things. I could live an exciting life.

ACTION STEP: What do you REALLY want? Are you living the life you want? In this one *moment,* right now, you can decide to change. You can decide that you are tired of *not living* your life. You deserve more. You deserve better. Once you decide, you're on your way. You have taken the toughest step – the *first* step.

What are you tired of in your life? What do you want to change? When you look back on your life, what do you want to have done?

_____

_____

_____

_____

_____

_____

_____

_____

_____

_____

_____

_____

_____

_____

_____

_____

_____

My moments had been building for years and it was time to take them out for a spin and put them to the test. I wanted more out of life. It was time to incorporate them into my life; to take a leap of faith. I was scared, but I was ready. So, with my parachute in hand, I jumped.

Follow
your dream

cʒ

Chapter 2

Believe in the possibilities.

"It's kind of fun to do the impossible."
- WALT DISNEY

This chapter has excerpts from countries I visited on my first Year of Action to give you a peek into what it's like to push yourself to follow your dream and to find the courage to live the life you want. It wasn't always easy but each day I felt like I was really living my life. When was the last time you said that?

Boston, October 1985

*W*e're taxiing down the runway about to take off. It doesn't seem real. *What am I doing? I bought a one-way ticket to Europe, with three guys? Am I crazy?* Absolutely. *Do I want to turn around?* Not for a second.

Often the hardest part is just *making* the decision; the back and forth, the pros and cons, the nerves, fears and worries. At some point you need to leap – to decide. Once you decide, things get a lot easier.

After I decided, I could start breathing. Things got a lot easier too once I had my plan. I started talking about it and I was committed. Plus it helped to say the dream out loud: *I am going to Europe!*

I was very lucky for two main reasons: 1) I was too busy getting ready for the trip to have any time to get nervous and 2) I had absolutely no idea what I was getting myself into. Ignorance *is* bliss!

The weeks leading up to the trip were a whirlwind. I quit my job. Moved out of my apartment. Moved in temporarily with friends. Picked up a freelance job - which helped me earn much needed money. Then the goodbyes started. There was a Goodbye Lunch at work and a big Surprise Party at Heather's. I bought a journal to write in and I asked my family and close friends to write something in it for me – for inspiration and for cheering me up when things got tough.

(Just to put things into perspective, in 1985 there were no cell phones. There was no Internet, no email, no Facebook, no texting. If you wanted to meet up with someone, you got a postage stamp. You had to make elaborate plans in advance and cross your fingers. You could try and find a payphone, decipher what the operator was saying in that language and hope you had the right (and enough) coins for a three-minute call. As far as money, there were no euros and very few ATMs. You had Travelers checks and you would exchange them into different currencies for whatever country you were in.)

So it wasn't until all the packing and planning and goodbye-ing was done and I was on the runway about to take off, that the weight of all of this hit me. My body started shaking.

I met up with my Loud Family travelling companions (Rob, Rick and Bob) in Newark. We didn't take off until 1 a.m. I had been up until 4 a.m. the night before and was exhausted. I fell asleep on the plane and woke up and didn't know where I was. Rob said, "Check out the window…sunrise over Europe."

It was beautiful. I was on my way.

ଓ

It was more than I could have imagined. I travelled for eight months and went to nine countries. I lived in London and Paris. I thought it was going to be an artist's tour of Europe with some French on the side. But this adventure – these moments turned into action – was so much more that that. Extraordinary places. Incredible people. Joy. Tears. Scary situations. Bonehead moves. Trusting myself. Overcoming fears. Moments that last a lifetime. Here's a peek into some of them:

Brussels, October 1985

The eagle has landed

We're here! We made it to Belgium!

None of us speaks much French - and when I say much, I really mean *any*. I was waiting in line to get train tickets while others were exchanging money. I almost stepped out of line as my turn was getting closer because I thought, "I have *no* idea what to say or what to ask for." *Year of Action!* I stayed in line.

Somehow I bought us tickets – hopefully to Brussels - and I picked up some maps. (No Google Maps back then either.) We met a nice woman who told us about a good, cheap hotel and showed us how to get there. We dragged our tired selves to the hotel, climbed the five flights of stairs and collapsed. The adventure has started.

Amsterdam, October 1985

Lust for Life

"Great things are done by a series of small things brought together."
                    - Vincent van Gogh

There is an entire museum dedicated to one of my favorite artists, Vincent van Gogh. I had a dream that a storm was coming and we were being evacuated and I had to leave Amsterdam before I could get to see the van Gogh museum. I said I wasn't leaving. I would stay through the storm. I have to see van Gogh! I woke up and realized it was only a dream. I WOULD get to see van Gogh!

I couldn't believe I was standing in front of his paintings. It hit me – his hands painted what was right before my eyes. It made me feel like we were connected somehow - in the same space.

It kind of knocked the wind out of me to see these paintings that I love. To be right in front of these works was such a great feeling. I was in my glory. It is like meeting a rock star or one of your heroes. I was really here. I was doing what I had only dreamed of.

ACTION STEP: You need to freeze those moments when you are doing what you never thought you could do. Write it down. Take a picture. Collect a ticket stub – something to see or touch - that you can use later as a tangible reminder of the possibilities, when you doubt yourself in the future!

Füssen, November 1985

The Castle

I just had my first glimpse of the Alps. Am I really here? It is absolutely breathtaking. We hiked up to see the Neuschwanstein Castle. As we climbed through the Alps it started getting really cold. We got to the castle and took the tour to warm up - even though it was only in German. Luckily Rob translated: *"This is where the trampoline was... The King's favorite meal was fluffernutter... He invited daVinci over and his favorite meal was grilled cheese...."*

AS WE WERE leaving Garmisch-Partenkirchen, the hotel owner didn't know how to process AmEx and we didn't have enough deutsche marks. She said her husband was the only one who knew how to use the credit card machine and he wouldn't be back for a few days.

I explained that we changed most of our deutsche marks because we were leaving the country. I told her that *I* knew how to use the AmEx machine. It was easy. Her son (macho) then said, "I can do it." She took what we had for DM and took American Express for the balance. But now we had no money for dinner. (Perhaps I could sell her some stamps!)

Venice, November 1985

Grand Canal

We walked the narrow cobblestone streets and over the little bridges in Venice. We saw San Marco during the day; so many pigeons. They sell bird food and people had pigeons all over their body. It was awful.

It is a different story at night. We went for a ride on the Grand Canal. It is so beautiful. Am I really in Venice? It was unbelievable to look at these huge structures and not see any land supporting them.

Venice at night has got to be one of the most romantic cities in the world. It is a little sad not to be sharing it with someone special.

Don't get me wrong. I am so lucky to be travelling with Rob, Rick and Bob. We've been having a ball. We are all very comfortable with each other and can talk about anything. They ask me for a woman's perspective on things. We are comfortable making all kinds of jokes. Talking about important things - life, relationships and why there were so many cats in Venice. (Looking back I was kind of like Elaine from Seinfeld.)

Florence, November 1985

Birds on the *David?*

I saw Michelangelo's *David* today in Florence! It is so magnificent. I don't know if it's because I've heard so much about it or what – but I have butterflies in my stomach. Can this really be a block of stone?

I am so happy. I've been learning so much every single day.

The city itself is a work of art. If you blink you might miss a masterpiece. It is overwhelming.

It is room after room of the most gorgeous paintings and sculptures that are viewed amid marbled floors, painted ceilings, velvet chairs, stained glass windows and chandeliers...

We walked ALL OVER the city. We went to the Uffizi Galleries - outside are statues of Michelangelo, Dante, Leonardo, Machiavelli - and *the David?* (I thought an outside copy was the real *David* at first and was infuriated that there were birds on it.)

Rome, November 1985

St. Peter's & the Sistine Chapel

It has been raining – actually POURING - the entire time. Someone broke in to our hotel while we were sleeping and robbed us. We were nearly ransacked by gypsies and *still* I think this is a magnificent city. That says a lot!

I will have nightmares though about climbing up the winding stairs into the Cupola (dome) in St. Peter's. It was so crowded and it is only wide enough for 1½ people. Yet people are coming down as you are going up, so it's a tight squeeze. Plus the ceiling gets lower and lower and you feel like you are in a dark cave with the walls squeezing in. It is so claustrophobic, but what a prize at the end of the climb.

"A thing of beauty is a joy forever."
- KEATS

Michelangelo's *Pieta* in St. Peter's is one of the most beautiful things I have ever seen. It is breathtaking. I couldn't believe I was there. This is what art is. It has a life of its own. It is so emotive and expressive. My eyes were tearing up. It is behind bulletproof glass now because someone tried to attack it with a hammer a few years ago. The thought of that is hard to fathom.

As I was reading over the things that have gotten me here (especially the things that make me nervous but I do anyway), I'm starting to realize that it is these learnings, these moments that are going to help me get through things in my life.

The art is magnificent, but what is happening outside the museums – testing myself, believing in myself, trusting myself - are the real treasures of this trip.

Salzburg, December 1985

*Ahhhh*madeus

Ahhhh. Salzburg. It is beautiful here and a healthy cold on your face. I'm loving it – singing and smiling and happy to be here. They are very proud of their favorite son: Wolfgang Amadeus Mozart. So much so they've immortalized him in chocolate. (There's also a statue.)

Strolled around and went to the Mozart Museum. Saw his piano! (Touched it actually – don't tell.) Five octaves, F to F, black keys with white sharps. His scratches of music, notes, hair (!), buttons, paintings, violins and operas all were there. It was so cool to be that close to brilliance. I imagined him sitting right in front of me at the keyboard composing a magnificent opera. I loved it.

Met a nice Aussie who asked me to a piano and flute concert at the *Mozarteum*. He plays the flute and we talked about music, art and being surrounded by it here in Europe. The acoustics in the *Mozarteum* were amazing. The flutist (flutist? flautist? "You say tomato.") was a real character. He was an engaging, rotund Austrian who, in the middle of the concert, stopped to give a dissertation on the flute. He showed us what the flute could do. Very avant-garde. Brilliant musician. Encores.

I am at a concert in Salzburg! I touched Mozart's piano today! *Ahhhh.* Feel myself breathing easy. Afterwards I walked around Salzburg at night – so pretty – very Christmas-like. Wreaths of evergreen, red and green hung across the narrow streets with white lights everywhere. Love it here. Went back to the hotel.

Had a beer with some new people. Talking about our adventures. Heard about people getting gassed and robbed on the trains in Rome. (I wonder if we were gassed in our room?)

I am becoming more comfortable with myself. I'm meeting so many new people.

Ireland, December 1985

Tracing my roots

When I was in high school, my family was a host family for a musical organization from Ireland. We originally signed up for one musician to stay with us, but when the group arrived, there were more people who needed homes. We took in two more.

We became especially close to one of the musicians, Peter. He reminded me of my grandfather. We stayed in touch over the years. I also had roommates in Boston from Ireland (Mary & Noel). They lived with LJ and me over the summer after Heather got married and then they moved back to Ireland (Macroom) in the fall.

When I started planning this trip I knew that the holidays would be tough. I had never been away from my family at Christmas. So the only plan that I made before I left, was to be in Ireland for Christmas with these friends - who are like family.

A highlight was getting to see where my grandparents were from: Cork and Cavan. My roots. I never thought I would get there. My grandmother was from a remote area (Glangevlin/Blacklion). It was eerie and moving to be where Nana grew up. The land was rocky with no possibility for farming. It is no wonder so many people left for America. Not by choice but by necessity in the hopes of a better life.

Her house was no longer standing. There were remnants and overgrown trees and brush amid the rubble. It was very moving to be in the same space - the same sights. She told me a story about waking up early on Easter Sunday to see the sun rise over the hills and saying that on Easter morning the sun would dance. I looked over those same hills and felt very close to her.

It is so peaceful in Ireland. *'Tis Grand.* The people are funny and genuine and loving and welcoming and trusting and musical and family-oriented. Their warmth is contagious and I found myself hoping to take some of their perspective on the world home with me. It makes me so proud to come from such good people.

London, January 1986

Covent Garden

Bumped into someone I recognized from Smith, Deborah, in Covent Garden. She is a law student here. I told her my friend had just arrived and we wanted to see the countryside and asked if she had any suggestions. She said that she had a car and would take us herself after her class on Friday. What an amazing offer! Yay Smith!

It was great to see London and the countryside with someone who knows the area. We went out to the Cotswolds and a cute little town called Burford. We continued on to Oxford. I didn't realize it was made up of about 15 colleges. We saw Christ College, Magdalen and Sighing Bridge. Went down by the Thames River to see them row.

It is great to be in a car exploring a city with a native. Much easier than the buses and trains!

We headed back to London and went to the "best Fish & Chips" place in London on Upper Street.

It is beautiful to see London by night. Tower of London all lit up. Crossed over the Tower Bridge. Down by the Houses of Parliament, Cleopatra's Needle and the remarkable St. Paul's Cathedral, created by our now dear friend Christopher Wren – after hearing the funny lines in *Mousetrap* about him. Also saw Harrods all lit up.

Paris, March 1986

Going to "The Show"

For an art major, there is nothing quite like being in Paris. I have been to beautiful museums in Boston, New York and in Europe. But Paris, well Paris is like getting to the major leagues, going to The Show: *The Louvre, Picasso and Rodin Museums, Jeu de Pomme, L'Orangerie, Musée National d'Art Moderne, Petit Palais, Grand Palais, Musée Marmottan ...*

Plus many are free. I would wake up and say, "I think I'll go to the Louvre today." I equate it with meeting one of your heroes or going to a great concert. I am inspired up at Montmartre with all the artists who are painting and sketching and I start sketching too!

This was my dream. I get to explore these museums – as often as I want. I get to sit in cafes with my pastels and capture Paris. I can't believe that I'm here doing what I had only dreamed of.

I love just strolling around the grounds of the beautiful Rodin Museum and seeing all the incredible statues like *Le Baiser* (The Kiss). One of my favorites of Rodin's is *The Walking Man* – a replica of this is at Smith College in the Hillyer Art Courtyard. (It was mercilessly dressed up in diapers, streamers, etc. by stressed out undergrads during exams. Sorry, Monsieur Rodin.)

I have loved seeing the Impressionists like the Degas dancers or works like Jacques-Louis David's, *The Coronation of Napoleon* – with the ornate details in the robes that make you feel like you can reach out and touch the velvet.

27/4

22:10

It's amazing to get to study these works in person.

Paris, April 1986

I love Paris in the springtime

The days are blurred. I met Thierry one night as I was coming back from a great dinner. I was so happy and not looking for anything. I guess it *does* happen when you least expect.

I'm being swept off my feet. We've seen each other nearly every day for a while now. He is very cool. Very nice. I love listening to him speak French. Strolling along the bridges at night. He told me he'd have to write and thank his English teachers. (I still have to bring a French dictionary on our dates.)

I am so happy. I have been trying to just enjoy this time while it lasts. I don't plan on staying in Paris forever. It is hard to keep that in perspective though. It is springtime in Paris after all!

We had an amazing whirlwind romance. None of this would have happened if I had held on to the relationships in my life that I knew weren't right. I had to let go. It was tough at the time but letting go opened up an adventure of a lifetime. Motorcycle rides and all.

Can it be that little Erin Moran from Worcester is parading around Paris? It is hard to believe. I'm actually here aren't I? When I think back to October and how I wondered what this would be like, I could have never imagined it. If I hadn't done this I would've regretted it ALL MY LIFE. Especially if I ever found out what it was like over here and what I was missing.

You can do it too

These pages are my proof to help convince you that anything is possible. I didn't have much to start. I didn't speak the language. I didn't have much money. I didn't know anyone. I didn't know anything about travelling. I was afraid but I just started. I took action. I did something. I took a step...and then another one. Then the momentum took over. It carried me through the nerves. Plus, it started to get easier when I started to act. That's all it takes. A step.

You *can* do what you want to do. You don't have to do it all at once. You first just need to *decide* you want to change. Then it's about doing little things that move you in that direction. But most importantly, you need to believe that you can do it. It's okay if you have to "fake it 'til you make it." With each little success, you will start to believe (and have proof) that it *is* possible. You will start to realize that you in fact, *can* do it.

At the beginning it was hard for me to believe that it would really

happen. But believe anyway. It *should* be a stretch of your imagination and it's okay to be afraid.

Dream big and be specific.

I am going to go to Paris.
I am going to see all the art I have loved.
I am going to learn to speak French.
I am going to travel to places that I have only dreamed about. Other people do it, why not me? It IS possible. I can do it!

(That's me on the Eiffel Tower. Small steps. Big life. *Year of Action.*)

ACTION STEP: YOU can take action right now to start living your BIG, fabulous life. On these next pages, write down some crazy, colossal, 'you've got to be kidding me', scary, fabulous dreams - even if they seem impossible and out of reach. Let yourself go. Let yourself dream.

Think of things that make you happy and make you feel alive. What has been in the back of your mind? Don't censor anything - just let yourself dream. It can be anything from cleaning out the garage to buying a house on the beach. Big dreams and small dreams - and be specific. You are on your way!

ACTION STEP: Look through your list of dreams. Say them out loud. Pick 3 dreams that you want – truly, honestly want - to happen. (Even if they seem completely out of reach.)

Pick 3 dreams you REALLY want. Pick ones that are important to you – even if they seem impossible.

1)

2)

3)

WHY? WHY are these dreams important to you? WHY do you want them? What would your life be like if you took action and made them happen?

1)

2)

3)

Chapter 3

You do belong here – but you have to actually *do* the work!

"The big secret in life is that there is no big secret.
Whatever your goal, you can get there if you're willing to work."
– OPRAH WINFREY

―――――――

It may sound like living your dream is easy. It's not. In fact, often it is quite
tough – and scary. But you are living your dream. Let me repeat that: YOU
ARE LIVING YOUR DREAM! It should be a little tough. This section
highlights some of the work that it took for me on my Year of Action abroad.

Brussels, October 1985

I still can't believe I'm actually doing this. I hadn't even dared to
dream about this. I didn't think someone "like me" could ever do
something like this. It seemed too out of my reach - something that
only other people, brave people, rich people could do. Yet here I am!

We walked the cobblestone streets and the Grand Place and feasted
on *les moules* – mostly so we could say we had *mussels in Brussels*. My
stomach was upset from so many things – jet lag, new foods, nerves. I
was afraid to ask directions, afraid to talk to people. It's scary when all
of a sudden the world as you know it, is gone. What am I doing here?

I decided being afraid wasn't going to work. This was my *Year of Action*. I needed to get over my fears. I started forcing myself to change.

Part of the adventure is meeting (and talking) to new people - even if you don't know the language. It's the people who are going to make this trip memorable.

For example, I met a young couple who told me that they had been out shopping. They came upon a little store with beautiful clothes and started browsing. They thought the owner seemed upset but they kept going through the racks. Then the owner started yelling at them and they had no idea what he was saying. They ended up leaving without buying anything. It was only later that they realized they were at a dry cleaners!

Munich, November 1985

Drücken and ziehen

Continuing my quest to speak to the locals, I learned a few phrases – Erin's phonetic German – not to be confused with actual German: *Excuse me:* Ent shuldigunk; *Can you help me?*: Helfen z meer bitah; and *How much is this?:* Viehere costed das.

Or when in doubt, you can just say "bitte" (bit-ah) which as far as I can tell means practically everything: *thanks, please, you're welcome, can I help you* and *please pass the strudel.*

These next two words will save you from much embarrassment: *drücken* means *push* and *ziehen* means *pull.* (There is no way to NOT look foolish when you walk up to a door and give it a hearty push only to realize there is a big sign instructing you to pull.)

As much as I am learning about others, I am really learning about myself. Once you take away everything that is familiar, you have to start reacting to completely new surroundings and situations. I don't know the language, the area, the money or the people, yet I found ways to adapt. I had to learn to not worry about being embarrassed or what others thought. I became good at sign language, smiling and learning the basics: *please, excuse me, can I, how much, where is, bathroom, 1-10, quick math for the exchange rate, thank you.*

Florence, November 1985

Italian leather

I was looking around the open marketplace for a leather jacket. For the first time, I was without my male escorts in Italy. I was a woman alone.

I couldn't get a coat fast enough. I felt so uncomfortable with the stares and remarks. *"Your mama did a good job."* *"Sssss sssssss."* You can't look at anybody and have to assume a tough exterior.

I found a jacket. It was just what I wanted. Tried it on. So soft. I loved it. The button was loose so I asked them to fix it for me. There were three guys manning the booth.

One told me I looked very lovable, licked his lips and stared at me. I started to feel uncomfortable. What is taking so long to fix a button? I got the coat. One guy said, "Can I give you a hug?" Before I could say anything, he did. I slipped away and started to go back to the main area. He came up behind me and put his arms around me and said, "I want to take you home. I think you are very sexy." I tried to get away and I couldn't. A shot of panic went right through me. Oh My God – I can't get away! He had a tight grip on me. And this was in broad daylight. I finally broke free and got away. It shook me up.

It made me think seriously about travelling by myself. There's a lot to think about being a woman on your own. If you are walking on a deserted street and see a group of men, it can be frightening. You can't let it stop you from living but you need to pay attention and be smart.

Somewhere near Vienna, December 1985

Unter-Purkers- what?

What a night. I have been travelling on my own for a couple of weeks. I heard the conductor say "Wein" (Vienna) and I gathered my stuff together quickly and got off the train.

It was pitch black. It was only when I was outside and off the train that I realized I had gotten off at the wrong stop. It was too late. The doors had closed and I was in the middle of nowhere, by myself in a nearly abandoned train station outside in the freezing cold rain.

There was no "station" with benches or an overhead shelter. There was no bathroom. There was just a small shed (like in the movie *Stripes* when Bill Murray goes in to rescue his platoon in East Germany). But hallelujah there was a ticket guy in the shed!

I went up to the tiny shed with the tiny window and asked the ticket man if I could get on Train #46 from there.

He said, "That's in Vienna."

"Isn't *this* Vienna?"

"No this is Unter-Purkersdorf."

"What???"

Then my only hope, my little ticket guy, shut the window in my face. There I was, pitifully standing out in the cold rain by myself in the pitch black with nothing in sight. Literally nothing in sight.

Where the *$#!% am I?

Unter-Purkersdorf, Austria.

I knew then that this would be one of those moments I would never forget. Later in life, when things are bad, I will think, "This may be bad, but it's not Unter-Purkersdorf!"

After an eternity, a train came. I just got on it. I didn't even care where it was going. I was getting out of here. And the wild goose chase continued. This train did take me to the real Wein. I ended up walking about 20 minutes trying to find a hotel. It was getting late. It was raining and cold. I was exhausted. My arms and feet hurt. I felt like crying. My throat was killing me. I hate Vienna!

Lost. Tired. Wet. Cold. Thirsty. Miserable.

I had to buy a bus ticket, but how? Oh, of course, at the Tobacco Shop. Then I got on the bus going the wrong way. No one spoke English. Then it started to seem funny. Somehow I finally got to a hotel. I have never felt so happy to get into a bed. I should have known when I dropped my pajamas in the shower this morning it was going to be a crazy day. It can only get better, right?

IT GOT BETTER. Much better!

I went to the breathtaking *Kunsthistorisches Museum*. I was thinking of what my favorite painting was. The first one that came to mind was *Jupiter and Io* by Correggio but I had no idea what museum it was in. I figured it was in Rome or Florence and was a shame I had missed it. I looked in a main *saal* and saw a Raphael and went in.

I turned the corner and there it was: *Jupiter and Io!* I couldn't believe it. I just thought of this and here it was! And *today* is Friday the 13th? Are you sure it wasn't *yesterday?* Maybe it's a time change thing.

Anyway, one of the reasons I love this painting is that you have to look closely. There is a man's face hidden in the clouds and a hand in the cloud wrapped around her. It is the story of Jupiter, a Greek God, who disguised himself as a cloud so he could sneak down to Earth and see his beloved, Io. Getting to see this up close was amazing! If I hadn't ventured out on my own, or if I had given up last night at Unter-Purkers*whatever*, I would never have seen this.

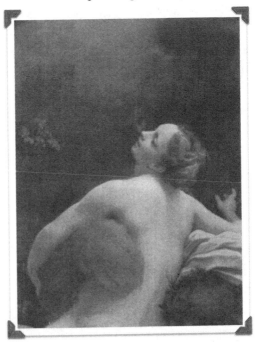

London, January 1986

Men, midnight rides and Moroccan drug dealers

I got a job waitressing at a restaurant in Piccadilly Circus. All of a sudden men started asking me out – to discos, to coffee, to live with them! I also seem to be a Tunisian, Algerian and Moroccan magnet – although I have no idea why!

I feel very safe in London. I ride the Tube after work at midnight (or later) without a problem. Well, except for the occasional homeless man and drug dealer.

One late night after work, I was sitting by myself waiting for the train. There are rows with about 20 seats bolted to the walls. I was the only one there. A homeless man came up and instead of taking *any* of the other vacant seats, he sat next to me and stared into my right cheek about an inch away from my face. He didn't say a word. But his nose was practically touching my cheek. I pretended to be enthralled with the wall plaster. It is funny now – and soon enough the train came.

Less funny was the Moroccan I met one night after work. I was too tired to lie to him and when he asked, I told him where I worked. He came in the next night. I wasn't working. One of my co-workers recognized this guy and asked him, "What are you bothering her for?" Turns out that *Mr. Morocco* is a big drug dealer. My friend told the staff that if that guy comes in again to tell him that I quit.

He came in again. This time, I was in the front of the restaurant. He saw me. I got so nervous. Told him I couldn't see him. He was persistent. I was nice but held my ground. He left. I didn't want him to be mad at me. I was worried he might be at the Tube late at night, since he knows which train I take. He wasn't.

Paris, March 1986

I can't do this

I've been feeling discouraged and "unconfident." It is tough. I don't know what I want to do here. I don't speak the language. I'm running out of money and I have to make some decisions and soon.
What is this trip all about?

I want to see what I'm made of. I have removed the world as I know it and want to see the type of person I am and how I function. I want to feel proud of myself. I want to face my fears. I don't want to be so afraid of things. I want to be living my life!

I think I'll have to leave Paris soon though. I need to do something besides worry. Some plan of action instead of just sitting around watching my money burn through my fingers.

There are so many discouraging brick walls and I don't know if they are signs to leave or to fight harder. Well, I'm going to sleep on it.

I'M SITTING IN a café on Rue du Rivoli watching Paris walk by. Things seem a lot different today. I went to bed last night feeling defeated and afraid. I couldn't communicate with anyone and I felt so helpless and stupid and depressed. It was too hard.

When I walk around Paris by the Seine, I remember why I want to be here. I love it here. I don't have to feel so afraid. Fears just don't disappear; you have to chase them away.

I made a plan of action. I want to stay. I want to find an au pair job and learn French. I bought myself a great French language book.

(The *next* day was when I got my apartment and job. I would have my own studio apartment and free monthly Metro pass in exchange for watching a ten-year-old girl from 4 to 6 p.m. Monday-Friday. It was perfect! I came SO close to giving up and little did I know how close I was to getting exactly what I wanted – if I just did the work.)

I have a place in Paris overlooking the Eiffel Tower. I am living my dream!

ACTION STEP: What's stopping you? On the left side below, list what's stopping you from taking action on your dreams. On the right side, write possible solutions. (You don't have to know the exact solution, just what are *possible* solutions.)

Things that are in my way

What can I do? Who can help?

I don't speak French	→	*Buy a French dictionary*
	→	
	→	
	→	
	→	
	→	
	→	
	→	
	→	
	→	
	→	
	→	
	→	
	→	
	→	
	→	
	→	
	→	

Chapter 4

You're no fun anymore!

"You don't stop laughing because you grow older.
You grow older because you stop laughing."
– MAURICE CHEVALIER

Laughter is key. You can't take yourself or things too seriously. You need to be able to laugh at yourself and take a deep breath. You also can't worry about looking like an idiot. Life is short – have some fun!

Munich, November 1985

*W*e headed back to the *Marienplatz* for dinner. It takes us a long time with the menus and ordering. We don't know what anything is. I decided that I would be adventurous and just pick something that I had NO idea what it was. I ordered it and then asked the waiter, "What is that anyway?"

He replied in a thick accent, "It is, how you say, the brain of a cow."

"On second thought, I'll just have the noodles."

Munich, November 1985

The Hofbräuhaus

The *Hofbräuhaus* is a big party. You pull (ziehen!) heavy carved doors and enter into a bright circus environment with loud happy music and loud happy patrons - perfect for the Loud Family. You sit at tables with lots of new people. As soon as we sat down, people started talking and laughing with us. We got beers before we could say, *"Guten Abend."*

Our waitress, a little woman of about 60, with tiny, bony arms could carry *six* steins - in one hand! The glasses are huge and heavy. I could barely lift *one*. A guy asked me to dance up front by the band. You haven't lived until you do the chicken dance at the *Hofbräuhaus* with an Oompah band. Another guy asked me for my address and I gladly gave it to him: *1600 Pennsylvania Avenue, Washington DC.*

We had a great, fun night.

We hopped a train to Innsbruck. We saw an Innsbruck sign and got off. A woman came running after us saying, "Nicht bahnof, nicht bahnof!" We nodded and got off the train.

As we watched the train pull away we realized that *nicht bahnof* means, "It's *not* the train station." (Perhaps THAT would have been a better phrase to learn than "push" and "pull.")

Paris, November 1985

Où est la Tour Eiffel?

We rode the slanted elevator up to the third floor – and got a fabulous view of Paris. **I am on the Eiffel Tower!** Can I really be here? I never thought I would get here.

It is so different to see the Eiffel Tower in person. It is HUGE and very cool to stand underneath and look up into the center of it.

There are 2,500,000 rivets and 50 tons of paint. (I learned this from sitting through two showings of the free movie in the warm theater with comfortable chairs.)

I also learned about Franz Reichelt the tailor who invented a "flying suit" – albeit a bad one - and he was killed testing it out by jumping off the Eiffel Tower in it.

Rob challenged me to a dare. (Not involving a flying suit.)

I accepted.

I went up to a street vendor *directly underneath* the Eiffel Tower and said, "Pardon Monsieur, où est la Tour Eiffel?" (Excuse me sir, where is the Eiffel Tower?)

He looked at me and smiled and said, "Hmmm...La Tour Eiffel? La Tour Eiffel? Je ne sais pas." (I don't know.) My brother would be proud.

ଓଃ

You need to find fun in the everyday. Not take yourself too seriously. We will be walking through a museum, admiring the paintings and then pretend to knock it off the wall or laugh at the crazy outfit in the painting or make a joke about what they were thinking while they were painting it. (They seemed to have left these important facts out of the Art History courses at Smith.)

When the tour guide said, "You must make sure that you get to the exhibit right away," we turned and immediately raced down the stairs! We have a blast making a game out of life and enjoying all the little things, enjoying all that is around us and enjoying each other.

Paris, November 1985

That statue is moving!

We went to the Louvre to see a 19th century pastel exhibition. After some searching (at the other end of the museum – and going outside), we found the pastel exhibit with Delacroix, Boudin, Degas and Manet.

We did have to stop in the Tuilleries outside to climb up on empty pedestals and pose as statues. People were waving and laughing.

Monte Carlo, December 1985

Winner, winner, ~~chicken~~ *couscous* dinner

Monte Carlo is spectacular. Very posh. The casino is across from one of the most expensive hotels in the world, *Hotel de Paris*. We walked into the casino and pretended that we knew what we were doing. We had no idea.

We watched Black Jack and burned through 100 francs in minutes with a few spins of the Roulette wheel. I had 20 francs that I turned into single coins so I could shake it in a cup and feel like a winner.

I found a slot machine. My first pull I got three in a row but I didn't understand the directions or what the machine was saying. I didn't get any money but the lights were flashing. I put in another franc to see if that would give me my money. Nothing. I kept putting in coins and playing the maximum credit. The numbers kept building.

I looked at other machines and they had credits of 4 or 6...I had over 200. I started pushing all the buttons and then all of a sudden, hundreds of coins came barreling out of the machine!

I was taking fistfuls and filling up my cup. It was SO much fun! I won...*at Monte Carlo!* We went back to Nice for a late dinner. We found an Indian place. A little man greeted us and said, "Couscous fini." We thought he meant they were closed. He kept rambling on about "couscous fini." We were standing in the middle of the restaurant not knowing WHAT was going on. He motioned us to sit down and kept saying couscous. *What the hell is couscous?*

While we were still looking at the menu, he ran into the kitchen and came back with a huge platter of smashed rice and started dishing it out to us. Then soup. Then chickpeas and lamb on top. (When do you go to a restaurant and get served *before* you order?) C'est la vie.

We started eating. It tasted good at first but something hit me and I couldn't eat another bite. Strolled back to the hotel. My last night on the Riviera. *Ahhhh.* The south of France is beautiful. *Au revoir, Nice.*

Not so fast. I woke up in the middle of the night with a terrible headache and fever. I was so sick. *Couscous this.*

Paris, March 1986

Chocolate mousse

Just when I thought I was starting to blend in with the Parisians...

My Loud Family companion Rob and I went to an elegant restaurant. As we walked in, we saw an amazing chocolate dessert in a huge glass bowl – like the size of about three goldfish bowls atop a glass pedestal. We knew what we were having for dessert.

We spoke French the entire time. We thought, "We *so* belong here."

After a delicious meal, the waiter asked us if we wanted dessert and we told him that we wanted the chocolate mousse. When he asked if we wanted one or two, we told him one. How could anyone even eat *one* of these – let alone two?

He brought the massive bowl to our table. We dug in. We were scooping out huge spoonfuls of the mousse. The waiter started giving us the hairy eyeball. We were eating and scooping and enjoying. More dirty looks from the garçon. What is his problem?

Just then, he came over and took the bowl away. He brought it to another table. It was only then that we realized that the bowl was for the entire restaurant! You are supposed to scoop out just enough for you. And I am quite sure you are not supposed to eat out of the bowl directly!

So much for blending in! We got out of there as fast as we could.

 **ACTION STEP:** This is one of my "go to" funny moments that always make me laugh. Pick 3 things that always make you laugh and write them down. When you're stressed, go to "Your Funny Place." Close your eyes. Take a deep breath. Think of your moment and have a laugh. It will get you through so much if you can just remember not to take yourself too seriously - and to laugh.

Go to "Your Funny Place": List 3 reminders of things that make you laugh:
e.g. Chocolate mousse

1) _____

2) _____

3) _____

Chapter 5

Have you stepped back from your painting lately?

"We can complain because rose bushes have thorns,
or rejoice because thorn bushes have roses."
– ABRAHAM LINCOLN

This is a real gift – to be able to see things from a different perspective; to see the world differently. This trip let me see things I had never seen before. Once you take away all that is familiar, you have a new appreciation for things you had taken for granted.

Train from Amsterdam to Heidelberg, November 1985

*W*e're on the train to Germany. The guards come around to check your passport. We were in a compartment with a young German woman and the guards went through all her things. It was frightening. They opened up everything, went through the trash, under the seats and through her bags. They checked her arms for needle marks. We couldn't believe it. She said it happens all the time – especially coming from Amsterdam. I had never witnessed anything like that before.

It made me realize that I don't know ANYTHING here: how to get tickets for the bus/subway, how much things cost, how to ask for directions, phones, money, anything! Yet it's exciting when you figure it out. Minor accomplishments are major. We congratulate each other for boldness, mainly breaking the language barrier. We all have to take turns ordering, asking, calling, etc.

I feel like I am a shy person learning to break out. Asking for directions and asking for help from people initially makes me nervous but each time gets a little easier.

Paris, May 1986

Homeless

Just before I was about to leave to go enjoy a gorgeous day in Paris, I had to go to the bathroom – down the hall. My apartment door shut behind me and I was locked out. Not a franc on me. No coat. No Metro pass. Nada. Rien. The family that I was working for was not at home. Now what?

It was 2 in the afternoon and they might be home around 4 – to have me watch my ten-year-old charge, Meghan. If not, they would probably be back around dinner. Besides it was a beautiful day. I wanted to go down to the Bois de Boulogne anyway. I didn't have my book and pastels but I headed out.

Spring is certainly here. The park is SO close; just a few minutes from my apartment. It is like Central Park. So beautiful: lakes, waterfalls, ducks, canoes, dogwoods, benches, green lawns, flowers and happy people. Felt great. So peaceful. Not many people by themselves though. But that's okay I was completely enjoying the day. Walked so much. Watched the motorized boats. About 4 o'clock I headed back home. I was even locked out of my entrance. Nobody home. Hit by a wave of exhaustion. Could hardly keep my eyes open. Took a catnap on the stairs. Felt pitiful. Still nice out. Walked back and forth to the Park. Fell asleep on the grass. Really fell asleep. Haven't slept much in days. I was exhausted.

About 5:30 I came back again. Getting nervous that "my family" was gone for the weekend. What would I do? No metro tickets. (Well I could always hop over.) Go over to my friend Tasha's – although I think she's travelling. If so, then what? I don't know anyone's phone number by heart. Plus, I don't even have any change. Where was I going to sleep? I had a jolt of what it must feel like to be homeless. It is scary.

I finally got inside my main entrance. I sat by the service entrance at the 4th floor. Waited. Listened for any sounds from Meghan's family. One of the sons came home and let me in. The family was going to be gone for the weekend – so I was very lucky!

Spring 1986

Quick recap

Some of the things I have learned so far:

I have proven to myself that I can face my fears. I am truly living my life. I am NOT letting it pass me by. Things that I thought were impossible for "someone like me" were suddenly mine for the taking.

It isn't easy. I didn't believe I could do all of this - even while going through it. I had never really pushed myself like this before. Never completely challenged myself. I was afraid. Things were hard…and frightening…and sometimes lonely. But I wasn't running away from what I wanted. I was running towards it.

I realized that I could count on myself - that I am self-reliant. I learned not to be so afraid of things and not to worry so much. I shed a lot of my fears - a big accomplishment.

Stepping back from my life, I can start seeing the person I am. I can start developing into the person I want to be - a person I can be proud of. It doesn't mean I have to run off to Europe every year. It just means that I have to stay in touch with myself to see where I am, what I really want and then make sure I'm not afraid to do what I need to do, to get it. I am changing my life. I have started living.

ACTION STEP: When was the last time you took a step back from your life? Try things that give you a new perspective on your life; things that highlight what you may take for granted.

1) Go to a new restaurant by yourself. Do not use your phone or read. What did it feel like to eat alone?

2) Visit a new area, neighborhood or city that you have never been to before. Make yourself talk to someone you don't know.

3) Volunteer at a hospital or nursing home or soup kitchen. (How big do *your* problems seem now?)

Chapter 6

It's always good to have a Plan B.

"You can't control the wind, but you can adjust your sails."
– YIDDISH PROVERB

No matter where you are in life, you need to be able to roll with the punches and have a Plan B. It's not about thinking you are going to fail with Plan A. It's about being able to stay cool when obstacles get in your way, learning not to panic and anticipating hurdles. Things usually don't *go exactly as planned – you need to be able to try something else; go around it, over it or through it. Find a new way. Know that there are other possibilities. Don't give up! A sense of humor is always good too.*

2011

I heard a story recently about a couple who had always dreamed of going to Venice. They had made elaborate plans and had been talking about it for months. Their trip was cancelled at the last minute and they were "stuck" in Amsterdam. This is where Plan B comes into play. You can either spend your whole time mourning (complaining) for what you *don't* have or you can choose to change course and start enjoying what you *do* have. Let go of Plan A and start embracing Plan B. Sometimes in life, you may think you want Venice but life throws you Amsterdam. (Guess what, Amsterdam is pretty great too – and has more canals than Venice!) It is up to you to choose how you react to it.

Paris, November 1985

What about Bob?

Rob, Rick and I got to Paris about 1 p.m. We grabbed our bags and made a mad dash to Napoleon's Tomb to try and meet Bob. He was expecting us around noon. We got there about 2. No Bob. *Trop Froid.* It was freezing. Now what are we going to do? We have no way to contact him. We have no idea where he is staying. We didn't have a back-up plan.

Rob went to the American Express office to see if there were any messages from Bob and to leave one for him.

(Before cell phones and email, we had American Express. You could go to an AmEx office in any city, show your credit card and then get/leave messages for people. You could have mail and packages delivered there too. It was a low-tech hub for meeting and connecting. It was our lifeline to the world.)

Rick and I were back at "Napoleon's." Outside. We were trying to think of warm things. I found a chocolate bar in my bag. Rick nearly kissed my feet. We hadn't eaten since 6 o'clock the night before.

We were freezing – and couldn't stand outside much longer. We tried to leave a note for Rob but as we were taping it on the pillar, we were told to remove it. We couldn't leave though because then we would lose Rob too.

Just then Rob came back. He left a note at AmEx for Bob to meet us at The Pompidou. We checked into a hotel and went over to The Centre Pompidou. It is high-tech architecture with pipes, scaffolding and tubing – but no Bob. We were starving and went to go get a bite to eat.

Walking along, all of a sudden Rob yelled, "Bob." Bob was across the street. He had never gotten our note and was idly walking around the streets of Paris. So unbelievable that we met. We listened to his Zermatt adventures. It sounded wonderful. We looked for a place to eat and sit and listen. My first meal in Paris was an American hamburger, but it was delicious!

I am in Paris!

ACTION STEP: When you are making plans with people, you should always have a *Plan B*. For example, "If for some reason we don't connect, let's leave a note at American Express saying where we'll be." Or "If you don't hear back from me, I'll just meet you in the lobby at 6 p.m." That way you don't have to make lots of phone calls back and forth (or if you don't have a phone – *or a signal* – you already have a backup plan in place).

Rome, November 1985

Roma, rain and robbery

I am travelling with two of my three Loud Family companions. We arrived in Rome late last night and I was excited to explore the city today. I went to get my contact lenses and couldn't find them. I remember putting them in my little black bag. My bag was gone. I started looking all over for it. I knew I had I left it on the chair but it wasn't there. I thought it must have fallen somewhere – there were three of us crammed in a small room and stuff was all over.

Then Rob couldn't find his wallet. I knew then that something was wrong. Someone had broken into our room – while we were sleeping! It wasn't just my wallet, but my contacts! I needed them! Luckily my passport and travelers checks were in a different bag so I still had them. But my money, credit cards and contacts were gone.

Rob found my bag outside behind sandbags. My wallet was gone but my contacts were there! We were talking to people to help us translate to police what happened. An older woman found my wallet in the trash downstairs. I got my credit cards back.

It was cold and raining but things started to look a lot better. To think that someone came into our room though was scary. We could have been hurt. What if we had woken up? What would they have done to us? Plus they could have taken our passports. I lost about $130 – which was a lot for me – but I feel very lucky.

We tried to proceed like a normal day. It was pouring. We headed towards the Pantheon. It was rebuilt by Hadrian about 130 A.D. and has a hole in the dome as the only light source. Raphael is buried there. It is beautiful.

 **ACTION STEP**: Have a default plan. Things usually do NOT go exactly as planned. The secret is to find ways to keep your cool when things don't go as planned or when you doubt yourself and are ready to give up. My whole trip itself was a big Plan B. When my friend backed out from going, I could have given up right there. But instead I came up with a Plan B – and went with new friends.

1. Remind yourself WHY you are doing this. Why is this dream worth the work? Why do you want it?

2. Go to "Your Funny Place".

3. Take out a reminder *(e.g. ticket stub, shell or report)* of when you did something you didn't think you could do.

4. Be open to exploring different options. You may have had one path in mind – but after taking action you can see that you need to try a new path – one that you had never even considered. It may be a path that's even better than what you had planned!

5. Don't waste time trying to change what you can't change. (I didn't *want* to be robbed in Rome or have it pour the whole time, but I didn't let the rain or the robbery ruin my limited time there. I took a deep breath and went out and enjoyed Rome. It was one of my favorite places.) Don't miss out on what you DO have by wasting it and focusing on what you DON'T have.

6. Go to Plan B.

Chapter 7

Some things are just a means to an end – do what you need to do.

"Everyone thinks of changing the world,
but no one thinks of changing himself."
– LEO TOLSTOY

It's easy to make excuses about why you can't do what you really want to do. You may have to make sacrifices, work hard, lose sleep or ask for help. I had to move out of my apartment, put my things in storage and be a nomad in friends' apartments for a few weeks. I picked up freelance work – one night staying up all night and working from 6 p.m. to 9 a.m. in a Boston office. Sometimes you just do what you need to do. It's not forever, it's just for now. It's a means to an end. No excuses. Just get going and get started. You'll be done before you know it.

London, January 1986

Isn't *this* the language I speak?

Everybody comments on my accent and my expressions. Even though it is the same language and all, there are so many different expressions and foods. They tease me about things like:

- *Pocketbook* - It doesn't go in your pocket and it's not a book.
- *Sneakers* - Are you *sneaking* around? They're runners.
- *Trashcan* - It's a bin.
- *Long line at the movies* - Long queue at the cinema.
- *Excuse me* - Sorry.

As a waitress, I also had to learn about food and drinks too:

- *Clotted Cream* – sounds awful, tastes delicious. It's a heavy, whipped cream to put over scones at High Tea.
- *Bangers & Mashed* – a popular breakfast item - sausages and mashed potatoes
- *Pudding* – dessert
- *Black Pudding* – This is NOT a chocolate dessert! It is a black sausage.
- *Pie* – A meat pie, like mince meat or the popular steak and kidney pie
- *Tomăto sauce* - ketchup
- *Chips* – french fries (So instead of saying, "Would you like ketchup with your fries?" I would say, "Would you like tomăto sauce with your chips?")
- *Crisps* – potato chips
- *Shandy* – beer mixed with lemonade

I also learned some fun *Cockney* expressions which are rhyming words: *Apples & Pears* = Stairs; *Butcher's Hook* = Look; *Slab of Meat* = Feet; *Brahms & Liszt* = Pissed (drunk).

The customers don't know what I mean when I say things like, "Are you all set?" (Set for what?) Or one of my favorites was from someone who was apparently astonished by tales of American cuisine and asked me, "You mean you have peanut butter and jelly...*together?*"

London, January 1986

She works hard for the money

So, once I figured out what someone was actually ordering I would have to run up 18 stairs to the kitchen to place and pickup my orders. Just for fun, halfway down the stairs was a landing where you'd have to turn. And in case that wasn't treacherous enough, it was dark with reflective, mirrored walls to throw you off while you are carrying large trays of food during a dinner rush.

One of my first shifts, during a busy "theater crowd" rush, a man called me over while I had a big tray on my shoulder and said, "These prawns are warm."

I had no idea what prawns were – and if they were supposed to be hot or cold. I also couldn't stop right then with my tray of dinners to be delivered so I said, "The chef's trying out something new. What do you think?"

Being a polite Brit he said, "Well, uh, I guess they are all right."

I said, "Great - I'll tell him. Thanks."

ONCE THE ORDER was in, I would run back down the stairs and make the drinks. (Really? They want me to put lemonade in the beer?)

I would work until midnight and then take the Tube to Turnpike Lane (11 stops) and walk a few blocks to my flat.

Yet, despite my ignorance of British cuisine and the "bloody crazy" place, I loved it! I was having a ball with my co-workers and enjoying the customers. I don't know if I have ever worked so hard – and made so little money! Plus they are killing me in taxes!

Paris, March 1986

My Paris Penthouse

A little bit about my apartment in Paris:

I thought it was unbelievable with its killer view of the Eiffel Tower and the swank 16th arrondissement location. It had a couple of hitches. There were 140 stairs. One hundred and forty. No elevator.

(I was in great shape.) Anyone who came to visit was breathless by the time they got to my home on the 7th floor – a poor woman's Paris Penthouse!

I had a sink, mirror and hotplate. I had a bathroom down at the end of the hall. If you saw the bathroom you would not be impressed. If I saw it today I would probably wonder how I did it. You do what you need to do.

I couldn't have been happier!

 **ACTION STEP**: Don't let the excuse of "money" get in the way of doing what you really want to do. Where there's a will – there's a way.

If money were no object, what would you LOVE to do? (Go to college. Start a new company. Work at a non-profit. Become a racecar driver.)

_____

_____

_____

_____

_____

I washed dishes in college, gave out peanut butter in a supermarket, moved in with friends, moved home with my parents, waitressed in London and babysat in Paris, to make my dreams come true. Don't worry about what people might think. You may need to take a job or do something that is "below" you to get on the path for where you want to go. Little steps for big changes. It is a means to an end.

There may be grants, loans, internships or other creative ways to finance what you want to do. Companies may have offices in countries that you want to visit and they need people to live and work there. Do some research. Ask others how they did it. Be creative. Just don't give up before you even start. Just start.

Chapter 8

Be not afraid. Push yourself to do the things you think you cannot do.

"You gain strength, courage and confidence by every experience
in which you really stop to look fear in the face…
you must do the thing you think you cannot do."
– ELEANOR ROOSEVELT

There were many times that I was afraid. I never thought that I could do this. I worried a lot. But with each little triumph, things got a little easier. This section shows my progression from being afraid of spending a day alone, to travelling alone, to living in Europe alone. I just pushed myself each day to keep going, keep doing and keep trying. I learned to start believing in myself.

Paris, November 1985

*W*e are spending the day apart. I need to feel more independent. Ask questions. Learn my way around town. It is scary – but it is what I'm here for.

I'm sitting in a café in Paris. I thought it would be good if I spent the day alone. I felt like I wasn't really testing myself – merely relying on others to get around. I was afraid of being by myself but that is part of why I am here.

I'm proud of myself for spending the day by myself. Proud of the little things like going to the Post Office and having to speak French so that everyone could hear. Feeling stupid and wanting to leave, but doing it anyway. Finding my way around.

Nice, December 1985

I'm all alone

I'm leaving to go off on my own. I'm scared. It is not easy but it's what I need to do. If I want this time here in Europe to mean anything, I have to test and challenge myself. Otherwise it's just a prolonged vacation and not a test of who I am and what I am here for. I am sure there will be tough times on my own, but it is what I need to do. The test has begun.

As I watched the train leave the station, it hit me like a blast. Oh my God! I'm all alone. I just wanted to get somewhere so I could sit down and take a deep breath. As of this moment, no one in the world knows where I am or how to get in touch with me. What a strange feeling. I took a deep breath. I can do this. My flying solo has begun.

Geneva, December 1985

Strolling solo

I was strolling along the brick sidewalks of the *MarktPlatz* when a man came up and started talking to me. I didn't know what he was saying and I told him I didn't speak French. He started walking with me. We got to a street corner and he put his arm around me. I thought, "Don't make a big deal out of it, just relax and cross the street." We crossed and I took his hand off of me. He kept walking closer and talking to me even though I had no idea what he was saying. He kept staring at me. He put his arm around me again. I pointed to my ring finger (my gloves were on).

"Fiancé?"

I said, "Oui." (I had met a French poet in Nice who gave me that idea.)

We kept walking by the lake and I was upset that I couldn't stop or take a picture because when I would slow down he would put his hands on me. Even after I told him I had a fiancé he still kept trying to kiss me. I kept saying no and asked him to leave. He kept looking at me and saying, "Très jolie" and smiling. I tried to feel in control and not get nervous. He started again. That's that.

"No! I'm going back."

I just wanted to get back to the main street. Keep walking. You're fine. He put his hands on me again. Buddy, leave me alone. I'm almost to the corner now. I took a deep breath. He finally left.

My stomach feels kind of nervous, feel by myself – not lonely just alone and not sure of where I'm going tomorrow. It is definitely hard not to know anyone here.

Interlaken, December 1985

Ratatouille with Russians

Interlaken is a quiet town like Heidelberg. I found a place to stay and dropped off my stuff. My favorite part of the trip: getting rid of my bags.

It makes such a difference when you face your fears and when you challenge yourself. I am so happy. Just a little while ago I was by myself in Geneva and feeling alone and not knowing what to do and just wanting it to be time to meet my friends back in Paris. And now I'm hoping that I'll have enough time to do all I want to do before I have to leave for Paris.

A bus just pulled up, full of Russians. They want to show American, Swiss and Russian relations after the Reykjavík Summit. They're taking a photo of us for the *NY Times*.

Tonight we're all having *ratatouille* – whatever that is. Hopefully it's better than *couscous*.

Paris, March 1986

And then there was one

The last of my Loud Family companions has gone home. It would have been easy to pack my bags and go home too but I don't want to. That's a hard decision - but the right one. I want to be here. I am happy with myself for having the courage to come and believing in myself to stay. Another chapter unfolds. I sure am living.

It is sad without my friends but if I am going to be here, I'm going to give it my all. Get the most out of it. Dust myself off and go out and do some sketching with my new pastels. This might be just what I need. Keep greeting Paris with a smile. I am here, aren't I? This is the perfect final chapter. I will have to believe in myself. That's  what this is all about. I am making progress.

Paris, April 1986

Bombs on the Champs-Élysées

Thursday there were two bombs. One was on the Champs-Élysées that killed two people and injured 28. So horrible. One was diffused at Chatelet. When I used to read about bombs going off in different parts of the world, it didn't really sink in. They were faraway places. They didn't seem real.

But these are in my life. These are where I am. Often. It could have easily been me who was hurt or killed.

Heard stories on the radio about US and Libya but can't quite understand what happened. It seemed like war was imminent after

Qaddafi's tie-in with two bombs killing Americans. From what I can gather, the world is upset about the US attack on Tripoli. Three hostages in Lebanon were killed in response to the bombing. England let the U.S. take off from their air base. France refused. Nowhere is safe. Everywhere is a battlefield – busy streets, shopping galleries, embassies, cars, trains, metros and especially planes. People aren't travelling to Europe. Stepping over the shattered glass on the Champs-Élysées brings things a little too close for comfort.

There are three guards now at American Express. Going through my bags and pockets. American places are targets for terrorism. The dollar is dropping. Trying to decide what to do. Having trouble sleeping at night. My money is getting tight.

Paris, May 1986

It's time

I must say that I am very proud of myself for doing this; for being here. It feels pretty cool. It certainly hasn't been easy. In fact, it has been tough but I'm learning that that's part of the whole picture. There's not much satisfaction from something too easily gained. It's time though. I'm ready to go home.

Boston, May 1986

There's no place like home

We landed safely. I am back in the U.S. I can't believe it! Everybody's speaking English! I feel like going up and asking them where they are from. I can't believe how many phones there are and they all work!

I'm excited to be home but it is a culture shock. I feel like a foreigner. It is strange to have to readjust to the familiar. It is a shock to be back.

Mom and Dad met me at the airport. They looked fantastic. We had a great dinner. They helped me surprise everyone. My brother was graduating from college and I just showed up on campus and surprised him. I'm home!

So what have I learned?

This *Year of Action* way of living has been the best thing for me. I am believing in myself. I am learning that I am self-reliant and resourceful. I don't need to doubt myself.

I've seen myself come through some tough situations. I've been nervous and felt defeated and didn't throw in the towel. I had to call upon what I knew and solve my own problems. I removed the world I knew and had to depend on me. What have I learned?

Embrace the Fear

I learned not to be so afraid. Worrying gets you absolutely nowhere. I am a worrier but I am trying so hard to get over that. I have made HUGE progress yet I think it will be an ongoing process. I've gotten to a point where I know things will work out yet I still think a lot about them. It is always in the back of my mind.

Plenty of people want to defeat you – maybe not consciously – but they are doing it. They project their fears on to you: *"How will you speak the language?" "What will you do when you return?" "Why don't you just stay where you are?" "What if something happens?" "What if..."* There are too many *what ifs* to even consider.

Yes – there are realities that you need to consider. This is not about living in a *dream world* and keeping your fingers crossed that you will have enough to eat. This is about making a plan – even if you don't have all the answers and even if it terrifies you. It is about pushing yourself and living your life.

The unknown can be a frightening thing but it can also be exciting and filled with possibility. You chase away the fear by taking a step. Relax and breathe. Trust your instincts.

Believe in yourself

You have to remember to believe in yourself; to believe in doing what you know is right. You can't worry about how it might look or what people might say. *Be Not Afraid.*

I didn't have a lot in my favor – but what I *did* have was the heart and desire to go. All I needed was to believe in myself. The rest was easy – well, sort of.

Don't focus on what you *don't* have – but embrace what you *do* have. You *can* do what you never thought you could do. You *can* follow your dreams. You *can* do it!

Remember to freeze those moments or save a memento – a ticket stub or drawing – when you are doing what you never thought you could do. It will serve as a reminder as you go forward and continue to take action on

Notre-Dame
2 Mai
Vendredi

your dreams that you *can* do what seemed impossible! You *can* live a BIG, fabulous life. You have proof. Believe it!

Give yourself permission

I had no idea where to start. I didn't know anything about any of this. I didn't speak French. My friend backed out. I didn't have much money. I had never done anything like this before. I didn't know if I could do it. Deep down I didn't really think that I could do it. It would have been so easy to just stay put and complain about my life. I was afraid.

But, I gave myself permission. I started believing in myself. I didn't think about having to do everything all at once – that can be discouraging and overwhelming. I just started taking little steps. I went from tripping over posters, to finding out how to get a passport, to living in Paris.

What are you afraid of?

Everything. It is better to just keep doing what I am doing. Stay with what is comfortable. Things are fine. Adventure and joy are for other people. I'll do that later. I am not strong enough. I am afraid to try. What if I fall on my face? I am lucky to have a job. I can't take a risk at losing it. What if I leave it and can't find another job? What if I fail?

 **ACTION STEP**: What are you afraid of? What would you do if you couldn't fail? What is tugging at you to do? What is the worst that can happen?

What are you afraid of?

_____

_____

_____

If you COULDN'T FAIL, what would you do?

_____

_____

_____

_____

What is the worst thing that can happen if you try?

_____

_____

_____

Then what would you do?

_____

_____

"Remember, you can't steal second if you don't take your foot off first."

- FREDERICK B. WILCOX

Summary: Follow your dream

This section focused on taking a step back and seeing what your life looks like, believing in the possibilities, looking at what is stopping you from taking action and coming up with possible solutions. The *Action Steps* are exercises to jumpstart your BIG, fabulous life. (If you haven't done the *Action Steps* yet you can still read through this summary and go back to do the steps later.)

The *Action Steps* had you write down what you are doing with your life, what you are tired of and what you want to change. You came up with up a list of dreams – big and small – and chose three. You described WHY these dreams are important to you. It's not enough to say, "I want to win the lottery." It's about WHY. WHY do you want this? What would you do? Why is this dream important to you? Why will this make you happy? Do you REALLY want this? Why?

You came up with a list of things that are stopping you from taking action on your dreams, (i.e., I don't speak French), along with a list of possible solutions, (i.e., Take a class. Buy a French dictionary).

This section discussed fears and that it's normal to be afraid. You thought about what you would do if you couldn't fail and about not taking yourself too seriously and having fun along the way.

It talked about money being an *easy* excuse: *"I would do it but I don't have any money."* The truth is that if you want something enough, you can find a way. But you have to really want it. You have to be creative and open to possibilities. You have to do the work. It's not easy, but if you want to make it happen, money is just *one* of the things that you need to figure out. It doesn't have to be a showstopper. (I had very little money and I lived in London and Paris. If you asked me how I would do it before I left, I couldn't tell you. I had a plan and started taking steps and kept doing the work, little by little. Before I knew it I had an apartment overlooking the Eiffel Tower.)

Finally, this section had you start thinking about being an active participant in your life and giving yourself permission to start living the life you want. When you look back at your life, what do you want to have done? WHEN do you think that happens? It is not some magic day in the future – it starts today. It starts with little steps. YOU can choose to put yourself on the path to a BIG, fabulous life.

Later in this book, we will come back to your answers from these and other *Action Steps* to help you start to take action on your goals. These *Action Steps* are the beginning of your *Year of Action* roadmap. We will continue to collect the pieces and help you put them together at the end.

&

The next section focuses on how to go about identifying, experimenting and taking steps to find work that you love.

Find work
that you love

∝

Chapter 9

Take a step...
and then another one.

"Inaction breeds doubt and fear. Action breeds confidence and courage.
If you want to conquer fear, do not sit home and think about it.
Go out and get busy."
– DALE CARNEGIE

One of the reasons people don't follow their dreams or take action on their lives
is that they don't know exactly what to do. So they never start. This section
talks about the re-entry into my life when I got back from Europe. It's about
even when you don't know exactly what you are going to do, you just need to
take a step...and then another one.

Boston, September 1986

Jump back in

I moved home with my parents out in Worcester.

As much as it was great to be home, I missed my life in Paris. I missed the exhilaration. I missed the Seine. I missed...well everything. I spent the summer collecting myself and figuring out what to do next. A friend told me about a friend of hers who needed a roommate. We hit it off and I moved to Boston at the end of the summer and just jumped back in. I started doing contract work for a Spinnaker developer who had started her own company. I was doing computer graphics and design.

As I was rebuilding (a.k.a. broke), my brother Jim and I used to frequent some of the restaurants in nearby Copley Place that had Happy Hour with free appetizers. For the price of a drink, you could have dinner (and on good nights, enough for lunch the next day too).

My contract work turned into full-time and eventually into a role as creative director as the company continued to grow. I stayed at this job for a couple of years.

Meanwhile, I had been snooping around about some "real jobs" in Paris and had been in contact with the Musée d'Orsay – which opened shortly after I left Paris. They renovated an old railway station into a magnificent museum and now the Jeu De Paume and L'Orangerie had a real home to more adequately display the incredible works that had been crammed in tiny spaces.

I saw that the director was coming to the Isabella Stewart Gardner Museum in Boston and I went and talked with her. I told her my background and that I was interested in getting back to Paris and we talked about a potential position of developing software games for the museum. Over the next month we were sketching out a plan for a job. Then I got a call from my father.

He had been working on a program for elementary and middle school children about drug abuse prevention. It was integrated into the curriculum so teachers wouldn't have to take time away from other subjects to teach it. They could teach a few things at once, i.e., math, computers and alcohol. It was more than "Just Say No." It was about how to help students make decisions, teach them the facts about drugs and alcohol, about peer pressure, etc. It was a great program.

My father had gotten very interested in drugs after his heart attack. He had seen first-hand how difficult it was for doctors at leading hospitals to understand the exact dosages and interactions of different drugs. If it was tough for doctors, what are kids' chances who are experimenting with drugs on the streets? They need to know the facts and know how to make good decisions and deal with peer pressure.

The problem with the program was that it was all on paper and it needed to be a computer-based program. He asked if I could help him. I told the director at the Musée d'Orsay that I wouldn't be coming to Paris. I moved back to Worcester.

Worcester, September 1989

The Dungeon

Worcester gets some bad press. Mostly for the strong Boston accent, some sketchy neighborhoods and no direct access off the Mass Pike – making it a tough commute into Boston. But, Worcester was a great place to grow up. We had an amazing neighborhood. Great teachers. Phenomenal coaches. Active church and youth group. Wonderful and supportive friends.

Having said this, moving back to Worcester, after Paris and after Boston, was tough. Furthermore, my father had set up the basement as our workspace. Or, as I affectionately called it, *The Dungeon*.

Gone were the days of strolling by the Eiffel Tower or Le Rive Gauche. My new reality was sitting in *The Dungeon* looking into a paneled wall, with small glimmers of light coming in through the tiny basement windows. I had to keep rubbing my hands together because there was no real heat in the basement – just some space heaters. These would practically burn one part of your body while the rest of your body froze. I sat staring into an Apple computer creating a character we called *Digby* who took kids through a five-step, decision-making process: Find, Filter, Focus, Face and Follow.

I spent the better part of three years working on this project – with most of the first year in *The Dungeon*. We created a special version for the Los Angeles County Sheriff's Department and implemented it into 54 school districts (120,000 students) in California. Before we could implement it, we first had to run a pilot for a year. This required frequent trips out to Los Angeles and was the start of my fear of flying.

Somewhere over Los Angeles, September 1990

Fear of flying

"Ladies and gentlemen, this is your captain speaking. It seems that we have a problem with the airplane and we are going to have to return to LAX. We will keep you posted."

Not what you want to hear.

Before we could land we had to fly around for a while (to get rid of some fuel I think). It is very strange to be flying in a plane that has something wrong with it. Your mind is racing – but things were pretty calm and quiet. I remember some of the older people on board saying to their friends, "Well if I don't see you down there (on the ground), I'll see you up there (in heaven)."

Not comforting.

It was kind of a surreal fog. You are totally helpless and you just have to sit there for a long, long, time – it could have been minutes or hours – it is hard to know. Time just stops.

Flash forward a few years. I was on a winding road driving home from my sister's house. There were stone walls and trees on both sides of the road, with very little space to go anywhere. I could see out of the corner of my eye that a car was coming down a hill to my right. He had a stop sign but it didn't seem like he was slowing down. He kept coming. I realized we were going to collide – and there was nowhere for me to go. Everything started to go in slow motion as I slammed on the brakes and started to take inventory. I was glad when I realized that no one was in the car with me. I was glad that I had on my seat belt. I remember taking a deep breath. I prepared for impact.

To this day I don't know how we didn't hit. The man ran the stop sign and didn't brake. He should have hit me. I stopped short by about an inch of his car. I still feel like some kind of angel intervened and prevented us from hitting.

I was having that same kind of slow motion feeling in the air over Los Angeles.

The pilot came back on and told us that we would be landing and that we would see safety vehicles as a precaution.

After letting your mind wander about what is wrong with your plane (while you're *in* the plane), seeing fire trucks lining the runway is not comforting. It just makes it seem like you are going to crash. We didn't. We landed safely.

They fixed the mysterious problem and sent us back up in the air – in the same plane. As we were climbing, the pilot came back on and said, "Well...we thought we had it fixed but it looks like we still have a problem. We are going to have to land again."

What I heard was, "We have absolutely no idea what is wrong. We have our fingers crossed that we can land safely again."

I wondered how long it would take me to *walk* back to Boston. I was *not* going to get back on this plane. That is, if we actually landed. We did. But after having a couple of hours of being petrified into thinking that I was going to crash twice that day, I was shaken up. I got on a (different) plane for a third takeoff and made it home safely.

I also had a flight where we were just about to land in Boston – and instead of touching down – the pilot had to abort the landing, pull up at the last second and we had to take off again – because of wind shear. These *moments* would be hard for me to shake.

East Los Angeles, April 1991

A *Ride Along*

On one of the trips out to Los Angeles, a Sheriff's Deputy said, "We've seen what *you* do for a living, do you want to see what *we* do? Do you want to go on a *Ride Along?*"

"Okay." I thought he meant a ride around the block with the siren on. We would finish up for the day at four o'clock and he told me to go down to the Sheriff's Department and they would set me up.

I got there and I had to sign a bunch of forms talking about getting hurt or killed and I thought, "What have I gotten myself into?" Before I knew it, I was actually riding shotgun – meaning I was in the passenger seat up front – and there was a shotgun!

My partner was named Governor and he was an ex-gang member turned officer. He had a bulletproof vest. I didn't. He explained to me nonchalantly, how to call for help/backup if he got shot.

I was going to be with him from 5 p.m. to 1 a.m. patrolling the streets of East Los Angeles. This was where a lot of the kids lived, who were in our pilot program at school.

We were dispatched (that's police lingo for "sent" for those of you who have never done a *Ride Along*), on a number of calls. I thought the "domestic disturbance" ones would be easier than say, interrupting a robbery, but I learned that the domestic disturbance ones are tough because you never know what to expect.

They had just gotten new computers in the car and Governor and I made a good team. He drove and I taught him how to use the computer. He also had me use the high beam power light that was on my side of the car over my mirror when we were looking for someone. Sometimes I stayed in the car; sometimes I got out. I wasn't sure which was safer. (It made Unter-Purkersdorf seem like a cakewalk!)

The adrenaline rush is intense. The unknown. The dark. The sounds. I was afraid and excited. Wanting an exciting arrest and a quiet night. I got a little of both.

It gave me a new respect for what people do every single day to protect us. Putting their lives on the line. What an amazing group of people. Super *Action Heroes*!

 C3

When was the last time you tried something new?

I would never have imagined that I'd be working with drug prevention agents in Los Angeles. I just kept taking a step – and then another one. You don't have to know exactly what you want to do for work. But you don't figure it out by sitting around just *thinking* about it either. You need to jump in and start taking steps. Keep an open mind. Experiment. Try new things.

ACTION STEP: When was the last time you tried something new? Over the next month, try ONE NEW THING EVERY WEEK. Anything. Each week push yourself to do something a little more difficult. Talk to someone new. Drive a new way to work. Ask someone new to lunch. Volunteer on a new project. Experiment. Push yourself. Have some fun.

WEEK 1: This week the new thing I tried was:

_____

_____

It made me realize:

_____

_____

WEEK 2: This week the new thing I tried was:

_____

_____

It made me realize:

_____

_____

WEEK 3: This week the new thing I tried was:

_____

_____

It made me realize:

_____

_____

WEEK 4: This week the new thing I tried was:

_____

_____

It made me realize:

_____

Chapter 10

Give it your all – even on the little things.

"When I stand before God at the end of my life, I would hope that
I would not have a single bit of talent left, and could say,
'I used everything you gave me.' "
– ERMA BOMBECK

Putting a big effort into a small art project at Smith College lead to an
amazing apprenticeship with a world-class artist. This is a good lesson to
learn in life. Give it your all – even on the little things. You never know what
"giving it your all" will lead to. Plus, if nothing else, doing good work is
well...good work. Here is an example of where doing good work on something
little, brought worldwide attention to my door.

Boston, August 1992

*A*fter finishing the drug prevention program, I wasn't quite sure
what to do next. I hadn't been on an interview in a long time. I applied
to a job as a project manager in publishing. It was a "blind ad" in that
they didn't give out the company name until you actually got the
interview. When I found out it was at a legal publishing company (I'll
just refer to it here as *'That Legal Place'*), I almost didn't go. What do I
know about the law or working with lawyers? I went anyway figuring
the interview would be good practice.

In talking with the CFO, I realized how much this place needed me. The editors were just getting off of typewriters and had very little technology. I took the job and stayed for seven years. No one was more surprised by that than me.

I liked building something from nothing. Starting my own department. Building a team. Transforming old school to new school. Creating new products. One of these new products was taking the paper opinions that are written everyday from the courts and putting them online. We physically had people go around to the courts and pick them up, scan them, tag them and make them available to download. This was a big deal back in 1993.

Boston, November 1997

The Nanny Case

My brother Jim, *Mr. You're No Fun Anymore,* was great at disguising his voice. He could fake anyone out. Even me. He was always calling and pretending that you won a car, or that your suits at the dry cleaners had been ruined or your flight had been cancelled.

One year, on my birthday, I got a call from someone who said they were from the *NY Times* and they wanted to review one of my computer games.

"Oh really? The *NY Times.*" I thought I'd play along with this birthday prank.

After I gave a few snide remarks to my brother/reporter, I started to realize that he was asking questions my brother wouldn't know about. Oh no. I went pale. This actually WAS a reporter from the *NY Times.* Oh my God. What have I done? What have I said? I snapped to attention. I tried to recover and squeeze all my legitimate comments into the last few questions and just kept my fingers crossed until the review came out. Amazingly, it was a positive review.

You'd think I'd have learned my lesson.

Fast-forward a few years to me sitting in my office at *That Legal Place.* I got a call from someone saying they were from *ABC News.*

"Oh really? *ABC News*." (You know where this is going don't you?)

I started giving my "I know I'm being pranked answers" when I realized that these questions were not ones that my brother would know to ask. Gulp.

"Can you repeat that last question?"

I had no idea what this guy was talking about. What case? Why are they calling me? Then the phones started ringing off the hook. People were coming into my office. All the TV stations in Boston. Then *CNN*. Then the *BBC*. WHAT is going on?

Seems the judge in a big case had just told the world that he wouldn't be releasing his decision to the press. Instead, he would be putting it on *ThatLegalPlace*.com.

The case involved a young, photogenic British nanny in Boston who was accused of killing a baby in her care by shaking him to death. (The case went viral – before we even knew what viral meant.) It had worldwide attention.

The judge in the case was one of the judges who had us pick up his opinions every day. He didn't know about the Internet – he just knew that he wrote his decision and magically it appeared on *ThatLegalPlace*.com. To him, we *were* the Internet. The madness began.

It was 1997. Besides being an emotional case, it was a defining moment between old and new media. Most of the reporters I talked to were trying to hold back the horseless carriage of this new world; arguing that this newfangled technology couldn't stand up to solid broadcast news. All I could see was the panic in their faces and in their questions about what was coming.

Besides being personally thrust into the spotlight, as CIO I was worried about our servers crashing with the sudden worldwide attention. We typically got about 30,000 hits a month and we now were getting 800,000 hits a day! I quickly called around to set up some partnerships with bigger companies to help us handle the global load. I was in newspapers, magazines and on television. All because we had set up an easy way for judges to put their decisions online.

My connection to *The Nanny Case* didn't end there. A year later, when I was in labor with my first child, I was stunned when the anesthesiologist walked in. I recognized him from the news. It was *his* nanny who had been on trial. It was *his* baby son who had died.

He didn't know that we were strangely connected to each other. He had an aura of kindness around him with a very comforting smile. A gentle soul who was skillfully teaching a medical intern as well as making me feel at ease. You would never have known what he had been through. I know that for about two weeks, my life had been turned upside down being in the middle of a media frenzy. When I saw him, I thought about what his life must have been like during that time – while trying to cope with his grief. How easy it would have been for him to be angry at the world, to be bitter. Yet here he was, delighted for us about the impending birth of our child. A real-life, unsung hero.

ACTION STEP: Artists sign their work. What if you had to sign your work? Would you be proud to have your name attached to it?

Create something this week and "sign it". It could be a great report, a meal or part of a small project that no one is paying any attention to. Anything. Just give it your all - and sign it. Feel good about putting your name on it.

If you learn to start giving your all – even on the little things – you will be amazed at how good you feel – and at the incredible work you will start creating.

Chapter 11

Just be yourself.

"Be yourself. Everyone else is already taken."
– OSCAR WILDE

When you are young, the most important thing is fitting in – having the same shoes, haircut and clothes – not wanting to stand out. When you are older, you are expected to be unique, to be special, to stand out. The sooner you can figure out who you are and what makes you "you" – the better. You need to BE you, to be authentic and to believe in yourself enough to have the courage to show your unique self to the world. I was often the only woman or the youngest person – or both - in a department. I didn't try to be someone else. I have always just been myself. It's not always easy, but it has never let me down. This section has a couple of examples.

Boston, 1992 - 1999

You're lucky. Ted likes you.

The CEO and founder of *That Legal Place* was a very smart, very direct, very tough old lawyer, whom I'll call Ted here. He worked mostly from home. When he came into the office, people kept their head down and tried to stay out of his line of fire. (Think *The Devil Wears Prada*.) People were afraid of him.

I know this because the management team would meet every Monday morning at 8:30 and we would go around the table with updates. Every Monday very smart, very talented executives would keep their eyes down and say, "I have nothing to report."

Really? Nothing to report? No news? No concerns? No teasers of what you are working on? No recent successes? Nothing?

I wasn't that smart.

When I started at this job I wasn't planning on staying. I didn't know ANYTHING about the law and I asked a lot of questions without fear that I was *supposed* to know it. I also spoke my mind with Ted – which usually received audible gasps from my colleagues.

I remember the first day I walked into Ted's office, he had his computer mouse upside down and cradled in his right hand. He was a leftie and was using his left index finger to scroll the track ball to move the cursor. I walked up to him, took the mouse, turned it over and said, "Here try this – it's much easier." I certainly couldn't have been the first person who saw him doing this, yet no one else had said anything!

He didn't know what to make of me. I was a triple threat: I was the youngest on the leadership team, the only woman and I knew about technology.

He truly was a pioneer in the legal publishing industry and could see technology's potential but was often completely frustrated by it. I had a second computer set up, just for his calls. I would get a call that would go something like, "Why doesn't it work when I press *g*?"

To which I would say, smiling to myself, "Hello, Ted, is that you?" He would never say hello or identify himself. I would answer his question and then expect about another ten calls in a row as he continued on with whatever frustrating technology he was working on.

I remember him asking me a battery of questions where he was mixing the technologies, which made it tough to answer. Something like, "Why can't we have the modem do the searching?" – which would be like asking, "Why don't you use the screwdriver to mop the floor?"

As I tried to figure out how to answer these questions, he got increasingly impatient with me. He started slamming his fist on the desk - a slam with every other word, saying, "The judge will instruct the witness to answer the question!"

I just laughed.

I then took a breath and stopped answering his individual questions, which were taking us all over the place and said, "I think this is where you're frustrated. You want to know the best way to do x. This is what I would do…"

We had many sessions like this.

He would also send me articles he was writing. I would edit them and send them back to him. One of the publishers saw what I was doing and said, "You're editing Ted's stuff! Are you crazy? We never edit his stuff."

"Well, if he doesn't want me to edit them, he should stop sending them to me."

He kept sending them to me.

One day, after a few fist-pounding sessions, he emphatically told me about something he wanted to do. I completely disagreed and knew of an easier way. I tried something new. I agreed. Then I pushed back from his desk and as I was rising out of my chair to leave I said, "Yah, we can do that. It will take a lot longer and be much more expensive…but sure, if that's what you want, we can do it."

"Wait, what do you mean?"

"Well, another way to do it - that is faster and cheaper - would be to…" and told him my idea.

We went with my idea.

SO WE WENT back and forth like this for about a year. I assumed that he would fire me for my insubordination but continued just being myself.

I think the turning point was my saying to him, after another bout of frustrating fist-pounding sessions, "Ted I thought you were paying me to tell you what I know. If you want, I can hang my awards around my office to prove to you that I know my stuff. And you certainly don't have to do what I propose, but it is my responsibility to tell you what I know. You can do whatever you want with the information – but I can't *not* tell you. If that's *not* the case, let me know and I'll leave."

Finally, I earned my stripes. The 'triple threat' had earned his trust. I became one of his right-hand people. One of the best compliments I ever had was at a conference where he introduced me as "a jewel in *That Legal Place* crown."

So I had to laugh, when people around the Monday morning management table would say to me, "You're lucky. Ted likes you."

Luck, my friend, had nothing to do with it.

Newton, November 2000

I won't do it

During my time at an Internet startup, we went through extremely aggressive milestones and funding and launches. It was one of the best times of my life. I had an amazing team. We did incredible work. We met all the impossible deadlines.

We also had three rounds of layoffs.

Layoffs and firings are definitely the worst part of being in management. These are people's lives and there are some tough, awful decisions. For the most part, I understand that sometimes it is what needs to happen. And yet, sometimes, it isn't.

I had already had to layoff a number of people when someone on the executive team – I'll call him Bill - wanted to layoff a great worker. This didn't make any sense. We had made all the cuts we were asked to make. This wouldn't have helped the bottom line and we needed this employee if we were to meet our milestone. The real kicker for me though was that the guy they wanted me to layoff was expecting twins – any day.

Enough.

I talked it over with my husband. I couldn't in good conscience do this and was ready to fall on my sword. I couldn't live with myself if I didn't stand up for this. My husband supported my decision.

I went back the next day and told them that this was not the right thing to do and I wouldn't do it. They could lay me off instead.

They kept the both of us.

The guy whose job I saved never knew any of this. The next day he and his wife had twins. Part of me feels that the whole reason I was at this company was just to save his job. It felt good.

Boston, September 2011

Good girls

I have a sticker in my purse: *"Women who behave, rarely make history."*

There are lots of books out there about *Good Girls*. About *Nice Girls*. We don't get the corner office. We finish last. We don't get ahead. We are cursed. We don't get rich. We don't change the world.

"Don't cause a scene." "Be polite." "Sit up straight." "Don't interrupt." "Wait your turn." "Follow the rules." "Do as I say." "Be a good girl."

Sounds more like training a dog.

I think you can find a balance. I'm nice *and* I break the rules.

Back when I was 25 and all my friends were getting married, I was quitting my job and packing for a one-way trip to Europe. Not what all the good girls were doing.

Now on my 50th, I quit a high paying job in the worst economy we have seen in a long while and I feel *good*. (Great, actually.)

You have to break some eggs to make an omelette.

Start cracking – and don't forget to be yourself.

 **ACTION STEP**: How do you see yourself? How do others see you? Is your unique self coming through? What steps can you take towards bringing that unique self to the surface?

What 3 adjectives would you use to describe yourself?

1)

2)

3)

Ask 3 people what 3 adjectives THEY would use to describe YOU:

1)

2)

3)

1)

2)

3)

1)

2)

3)

Do people see you as you see yourself? Is your unique self coming through? Are you being seen the way you want to be seen? What steps can you take towards finding and bringing your unique self to the surface?

Chapter 12

It's up to you
to stand up for yourself.

"Act as if what you do makes a difference.
It does."

– WILLIAM JAMES

As children, we're taught not to brag, "not to blow our own horn." At some point this changes to "Tell me about your accomplishments" and "It's the squeaky wheel that gets the grease." In other words, you need to stand up for yourself. Keeping your head down, working hard and hoping you'll be noticed for your efforts, is not enough. You can wish it weren't that way – but it is. It doesn't have to be confrontational or uncomfortable. You can do this in a way that works for you – but you need to learn to do it. Remember, I used to be afraid to raise my hand in class or ask my boss for a day off – so I get that this can seem impossible at first. It's not. Here are a few examples.

Boston, January 1999

I felt like family with Ted (at *That Legal Place*). He was almost like a second father to me and I was also close with his wife. I was often invited to their home. When I was looking to buy my first house, he would go check them out for me and give me his feedback.

His daughter was being groomed to take over the company and she and I got along very well. In fact, I was one of only two people from *That Legal Place* invited to her wedding.

113

So it caught me completely by surprise when I returned from maternity leave.

Ted had passed the company reins to his daughter who was now running the show. She had had a baby a year before me and was working a flexible schedule with a couple of days a week at home. After seven years, I was hoping to have some kind of flexibility too when I got back from maternity leave. We went to lunch and discussed it before I left. When she asked me about my plans for maternity leave, I told her that I was hoping that I could work out something creative like what she was doing.

"Could I work a day from home?"

"No I need you in the office."

"What about working different hours?"

"No I need you here when everyone is here."

"Okay, well could I just leave fifteen minutes early to catch an earlier train? I could bring work home with me." (This would have made a big difference with the train schedule. I could get home at 5:30 vs. 7:00 – which is huge when you have an infant at home.)

"No."

I was very disappointed but I figured we could work something out when I got back from my leave. I had no idea how wrong I was.

Suffice it to say that I saw firsthand the messiness of maternity leave. It was not pretty. I had to get a lawyer. I ended up negotiating a successful exit strategy but I was shocked that it all happened in the first place. Not to *me!* Not to one of the top people in the company. I was like part of the family. I had been working my butt off there for *seven* years! (Don't they know 'I'm a jewel in *That Legal Place* crown?')

None of that mattered. It was business.

I thought about women who are not in a position of power and wondered how they would handle it. It was a rude awakening.

Cambridge, October 1999

The dot com bubble

After *That Legal Place,* I went to an Internet consulting firm. It felt like *Top Gun* for the web. These guys were rock stars. Cool office space in Cambridge. (Actually it was the same building where I started at Spinnaker. Yet Spinnaker was in the basement and now I was on the top floor.) There were pool tables and lots of snacks and long hours. The web was exploding. We worked on huge projects for major banks, Fortune 500s and innovative companies all with an idea how to make zillions on the web.

I thought I would love it. I didn't. They weren't quite sure what to do with me. I wasn't a hardcore engineer like a lot of my colleagues – nor did I want to be. It was kind of like economics at Smith. I could do it – but I didn't like it.

They would send me out to talk to CEOs about networks and architecture and systems. After all, I had been a CIO so I understand why they wanted me to do this.

But I liked the creative process. I liked the strategy. I liked bringing the projects to life. Yet, I wasn't getting to do any of this. Not only was I doing work that I didn't like, I didn't feel qualified. When I raised my concerns with my bosses, they told me I was doing great and not to worry about it. It became increasingly uncomfortable for me though.

Then the person who did the Resource Allocation quit and they asked (told) me to step in. Resource Allocation was a thankless job. You had to assign the project teams for EVERY project in the company; figure out what a project needed and who was available (with the proper skills). It was a nightmare trying to juggle current projects and find people to work on all the new commitments that had been promised - even though everyone was already booked to capacity – and all without any real authority.

This had been someone's fulltime job. I was asked to do this on top of my own billable hours, projects, managing my team and travelling to meet with executives. No additional money. I was miserable.

I continued to try and find a niche there that made me happy. In the meantime, I was so frustrated with not being able to know how to staff the project teams, that I devised a way to easily gather and identify the skill levels of all the engineers. It was a quick way to see who the experts were on the different software and hardware systems and who wanted/needed training on which systems. Before then, there had been no way to see who knew what. Plus things were always changing, so it had to be easy to use and to update. Other offices started using my system and the CIO took me to lunch and asked me to implement my system across all 23 offices.

It was a big job. I was trying to convince myself I could be happy doing this, when I got a call. It was a job offer from an Internet startup. It would be a cut in pay and a lesser title to do something I wanted to do. I jumped at it.

THIS NEW COMPANY had spent *millions* on developing a website that didn't work. They were starting over. I was now on the other side of the table from the consultants - like the ones I had just left.

There were many people at this company who were new to the dot com world. I spoke up, asked questions and offered solutions. I rolled up my sleeves and did what was needed. I was taking action and getting things done. I showed the executive team that although I had come in at a lower title and salary, I was clearly capable of more and deserved more. I asked for a big raise and promotion and I got it.

Boston, February 2007

You need to ask

Elaine, a friend of mine from a women's group, and I kept bumping into each other. I felt like something was putting us together for some reason. I went online to see what she was doing and saw a job posting where she worked that looked great. However, the job search had been closed. I called her and asked her what she knew about the job. She made a call and asked them to open up the search for one more candidate.

After interviewing with 15 people, including the president, I was offered the job. I had kept elaborate notes from the interviews and conversations. In my notes I had a certain salary listed with this job. When they made me the offer, it was substantially (thousands and thousands) lower than what I had in my notes as the salary range. They were a little surprised when I didn't jump at the offer. I told them that I had a different salary number in my notes. I talked with Elaine and she helped me negotiate and get the higher salary.

This is a personal mission of mine – getting women to ask.

An August 2011 article in the *Huffington Post* talks about the fact that women are still "not negotiating."[3] Women still earn less than men for doing THE SAME JOB; earning 77 cents for every dollar a man earns. This translates roughly into women earning an average of $10,600 LESS A YEAR than a man – for doing the SAME job! It's even worse for African American and Latino women where the gap is $18,500 and 23,800 respectively![4]

In general, women just take what they are offered. Men ask. Women feel that if they just keep their heads down and do good work they will be recognized. That is NOT how it works. You need to ask! I repeat, YOU NEED TO ASK! You don't have to be a jerk about it or start making idle threats – but you are crazy not to ask.

Or put another way, here is a powerful example from the book, *Ask For It: How Women Can Use the Power of Negotiation to Get What They Really Want*[5]. Let's say a man and a woman, both twenty-two and just out of college with the same qualifications are offered the same job for $25,000. The woman accepts the $25,000. The man negotiates his starting salary to $30,000. He opens a low-interest account for that extra $5,000 and earns 3 percent a year. They both average a 3 percent annual salary increase (but the woman's is lower because the man started out higher). Each year, the man takes the *difference* between what he would have earned if he had accepted the $25,000 and what he actually earns and adds that to the $5,000 account he opened. By the time he is sixty-five, that account contains $784,000 - more than three-quarters of a million dollars - simply because he negotiated that one time!

Typically women say that they are uncomfortable asking or negotiating. There are many great books and resources and people out there to help you.

ACTION STEP: *So what* if you are a little uncomfortable for a few minutes – isn't that worth thousands and thousands of dollars? At the very least, don't say yes right away. Always ask to take a day to think about it. You can have someone help you with your strategy during that time.

It doesn't have to be just about salary either. It could be different hours, a flexible schedule, more vacation, a bonus, a different title, a computer or cell phone, a parking space, an earlier review... But you don't get any of it – nothing – if you don't ask. So ASK!

Get some help from people who are good negotiators, pick up a book, do something. It is SO worth it. Think of me there with you cheering you on, take a deep breath and do it! You need to ask. *Year of Action!*

Chapter 13

Find what you love. You can figure out later how to make it work.

"Don't ask yourself what the world needs, ask yourself what makes you come alive. And then go and do that. Because what the world needs is people who are alive."

– HOWARD THURMAN

As I look back on different jobs in my life, I realize that they were often labors of love. I did work that I loved and that had meaning. Sometimes I created a job out of it and sometimes it was just to do good work. Often I did not have the end game in sight, I just followed my instincts and did what I felt was right. It was also important to know when to move on to something else. This has served me well. I have created work that I am proud of and experimented and tried new things. It has given me new perspectives and new ways to solve problems. I have been the main breadwinner for my family, so it has been a juggling act of being able to make money and find work that I felt was important. The following are a few of my life and work experiments.

Boston, July 2002

Breast pumping in a supply closet

Shortly after my second child was born, I got a call from someone I had worked with who wanted to see if I could help him at his new company. I told him that I had just had a baby. He said that I could work whatever hours I wanted. I thought I would just help them a little. I stayed for three years.

A *moment* for me happened one day when I was in the middle of an all-day investor's meeting. We had a packed agenda with limited "bathroom breaks." I was still breastfeeding my daughter and I needed to pump! There was only one bathroom for men and women to share. So with our limited 10-minute breaks, I couldn't tie up the single bathroom the whole time to pump. I snuck into a tiny supply closet (that didn't even have a lock on the door). There were fifteen executives about ten feet away, and there I was huddled on a box, with my back to the unlocked door, praying no one would need any paper in the next few minutes. And I thought, so *this* is having it all.

Of course, no one said it would be easy, and at the time, I felt lucky to even have the closet! But something had to change. What was I doing all this for? My heart wasn't in it. Then another *moment* happened. A different heart needed me.

Boston, October 2004

Henry's Hearts

It started simply enough. I was helping my dear friend Heather, who was planning a fundraiser for Marfan syndrome, which is a connective tissue disorder that can cause the heart to rupture. The event was for the opening of the Pulitzer Prize- and Tony-winning musical "Rent" in Boston whose playwright, Jonathan Larson, had died from Marfan just days before his show opened on Broadway.

Heather's 10-year-old son at the time Henry, my godson, has Marfan syndrome. The event stressed that getting the word out about Marfan was key. Yet only a handful of people knew Henry had Marfan. He was a lot taller than other 5th graders but otherwise looked perfectly normal.

I would cringe when I would see how uncomfortable Henry would get when people would ask him why he didn't play basketball or comment (joke) about how tall he was.

(As a reminder, it is NEVER a good idea to comment on someone's body – even with seemingly innocuous comments, like height.)

For Henry it was just a constant reminder that he had Marfan and that it was something he felt he had to hide. One day Henry whispered to me, "Aunt Erin, it's because of the Marfan..."

Just then a *moment* happened.

I didn't want Henry going through life whispering about this. I didn't want him to feel like it was something he had to hide or to feel bad about or ashamed. I had to do something.

I called my friend Sheila Shechtman, CEO of GiftCorp, a company I loved and had used for years for my corporate gifts. I asked her to donate gifts for the event and it got us talking. We created a plan where I could sell gifts and have a percentage go back to Marfan for research.

My brother Jim heard about the idea and said he would donate $5,000. *Hmmm.* I didn't want to "waste" this money on just one event. I sat down with Henry.

We came up with the concept for *Henry's Hearts,* where we'd use what people and companies need to do anyway - send gifts - to raise money and awareness for Marfan research. I asked Henry how he felt about not hiding his disease anymore; about being brave; about the possibility of other kids saying things to him about being different.

He thought about it. Then he said, "Aunt Erin, the doctors say that they need people to know about this disease. We have to get the word out. Let's do it."

A true *Action Hero.*

I had some money. I had an idea I loved. I could handle all the technology and design stuff. I had a gift partner. I had a cause I believed in. I had...to tell my husband.

At the time we had two young children. I paid the mortgage. I paid the nanny. I had the health insurance. I wasn't happy with what I was doing and wanted to do something else. I knew nothing about the gift industry or non-profits. All I knew was that *Henry's Hearts* was something I had to do. I knew I would regret it if I didn't try. It was October 2004, and the Red Sox had just won the World Series. Anything is possible, I thought!

So I jumped.

It is exhilarating to follow your heart. I loved telling people what I was doing. Each gift had a card that talked about Marfan syndrome. People loved the gifts and the mission. We got some partnerships with some big companies. We were changing a little piece of the world.

But more than that, I loved how this changed Henry. He was no longer hiding a secret. Marfan is just part of who he is. A highlight for me was watching him hand out *Henry's Hearts* chocolates at an event and when people said, "Wow, *you're* Henry!" a huge smile came across his face.

My hiding in the supply closet days were over. I worked out of a home office and could pick up my son at the school bus stop and have tea parties with my daughter. Most days, I worked late into the night after my kids were in bed. Every day was a new juggling act. But the toughest adjustment had been the money. Or the lack of it.

I didn't draw a salary for more than a year. This is *not* exhilarating. No money also meant no paid childcare. My husband and I staggered our schedules and did "creative childcare" with family and friends. It was tough. Money stress is tough. You have to develop a stomach for it and come up with options. I had to borrow money from family, which I've since paid back in full.

I picked up some consulting gigs and I had to ask for help. Asking for help was new for me. I used to think asking for help was a sign of weakness. I thought that you need to do it all by yourself. That's crazy! Sure, I probably *could* do it all, but it was killing me. Why am I doing this to myself? I *do* need help.

Now I think it is a sign of strength, not weakness, to ask for help. It takes courage to ask for help. Plus, if you think past yourself, it is easier. It is not about me. It is about raising money to help Henry and others, so I started asking.

That's been another gift. In relying more on others, I've realized how lucky I am. I have fabulous people in my life, people who want to help. I am a good friend to others, and I had to learn that they want to be able to help me back in return.

As I think back on my journey from the supply closet, I know it is not about trying to *have it all*. I think I had it all, and it was too much. Or maybe it was just someone else's version of having it all. It is more about taking the time to figure out how to follow *your* heart and make your life fit around that. It is not easy. In fact, it is very hard. But I was happy. I felt that what I was doing mattered and that I was setting a good example for my kids. I was getting to see them and I was following my heart – while helping to fix Henry's.

November 8, 2007

Blue blanket of love

Henry's disease, Marfan, is hard to diagnose. There is not one definitive test to detect it and there is no cure. Typically those with Marfan are extremely tall, have long thin faces, fingers and toes – and their heart gets extremely large. Imagine a garden hose (aorta) being stretched so long that it finally ruptures.

Henry had his aorta measured every few months. As he got closer to the "danger zone" they would need to make some tough decisions. Do they do a planned operation and replace the aorta? Do they wait and see? After all, it might never rupture. If he gets hit in the chest would that cause a rupture? Do you tell a gifted pitcher that he has to stop playing baseball? Each doctor's visit, Henry inched closer to the danger zone. Finally, Heather, Bill and Henry decided it was time. They scheduled the operation.

Studies show that *just* before going into surgery (while you are prepped and waiting to be wheeled into the operating room) if you can get yourself into the right frame of mind and in a calm peaceful state, your odds of success somehow are amazingly increased[6]. If you feel like everything is going to be okay, it can improve your success rate for the surgery and your recovery.

There is a *Blanket of Love* method that helps patients get into this peaceful state. Heather had heard about this and was determined to give Henry every advantage. You pick a color – Henry picked blue. You contact friends and family and give them a 15-minute window before the surgery and ask them to say prayers during that time. We were to imagine wrapping Henry in a blue blanket of love. Then, just before surgery, Henry imagines that he is being wrapped in a blue blanket of love from all his family and friends.

We sent the word out. I had people praying and thinking about Henry from New York to South America to Egypt, in churches, living rooms and office buildings from 7:30 – 7:45 a.m. EST. My kids and I sat on the floor in our family room, literally wrapped in a blue blanket, and saying prayers for Henry out loud.

When doctors and medical personnel walked into Henry's room they commented on the blast of heat they felt. They didn't know about the *Blanket of Love* but they could physically feel the heat in the room. Henry's face was flush. Something happened that morning. He truly felt the love. It was in the room. The surgery was a huge success. It was a great decision that they did the surgery when they did – his aorta was about to rupture at any moment.

HENRY HAS BEEN doing very well. He still needs to be mindful of his disease but he is leading a normal life.

A highlight for me with *Henry's Hearts* was at Cipriani's in New York. There was a huge Marfan event with Brian Williams hosting along with other New York celebrities. They were honoring Heather and Henry along with an amazing doctor.

There were more than 500 people there. It was like our Academy Awards. Henry was "out" with his disease. It was part of his life. We got the word out about Marfan. I felt like my work here was done. I wanted to find something new - and make a more livable salary.

Medfield, Summer 2003

Mural

During this time, I also took on a labor of love.

I love books. Shortly after we moved into our house, our town library was renovated. The Children's Room was beautiful – but had a lot of white walls and I thought I could help. I talked to the children's librarian to see if they wanted me to paint a mural. Since it was a new building, they weren't sure what they were going to do for the long term and she said, "Thanks, but not now."

A few months went by. It was a Thursday night and we had taken the kids to *Story Time* at the library. The librarian ran up to me as we were leaving and said, "I'm so glad to see you! We are looking to have designers submit their ideas for a mural for the library. And I wanted to let you know about it."

I said, "Great. When do you need the designs?"

She said, "Well…they're due on Monday. I realize it's last minute but I didn't have your name or know how to contact you."

I spent the weekend putting together an idea and presented it to The Friends of the Library Board on Monday.

The mural was for the two flights of stairs up to the Children's Room. It is about 30 feet long and 15 feet high. My concept was to use the architecture. You start "underwater" at the bottom of the stairs. As you climb the stairs you get higher up in the mural until you get to the mountains at the top of the stairs. The part I was excited about was I wanted to "draw" kids into the library by "drawing them" into the library. I wanted to paint footprints on the floor so kids could stand in them and be part of the mural. The Board loved the idea.

I painted the mural over the summer on weekends when the library was closed. I had kids help me do the painting too and I hid their names throughout the mural. *FYI – There are 15 names in the mural. They are hidden in the bear, fish, octopus, giraffe, snake and scuba diver.*

I love watching kids run up to the mural and put their feet in the footprints and giggle. They get their pictures taken with the mural when they get their Library Card.

Anne Russo, the children's librarian, was amazing during this entire process and we've remained good friends throughout the years.

They had a big unveiling party, created a plaque and dedicated 20 books to my kids that are in circulation and have their names on special bookplates in the front of the books. But the best was a book that they had been secretly creating. It had all of the comments from people who were watching the mural take shape over the summer. This little book is one of my prized possessions.

This was a great experience. I had never done a painting this big before and it was a little intimidating. I had to figure out how to get and set-up the scaffolding and what kind of paints would be best – especially for the floor.

I had to figure out how to best protect it with kids touching it and stepping on the footprints. I had to figure out how to map out the drawing on the wall. I asked questions and figured it out. One step at a time.

Los Angeles, 1991

Changing lives – a little.

The yearlong experience in Los Angeles with the drug program was another highlight of my life. It was a chance to bring my father's dream to life and perhaps change a few lives in the process.

I remember flying into L.A. and looking down at all the houses and thinking of all the kids in all those houses who were going to be learning from things that we had created. It felt good.

A more direct experience was seeing the light go off in a young child's face. These kids were streetwise and dealt with harsh realities every day. I wondered what I could possibly help teach them. We had been working on a lesson that talked about the effects of cocaine and I had created images of the heart to show how it was impacted. Just then something clicked for a young boy I was working with and he looked up at me and said, "Man – you could have a heart attack from crack."

"That's right."

"Whoa."

One life, changed - a little.

You are not your work.

You can be passionate about your work – but remember there is more to life than work. Nobody wants to be bored with endless tales of work woes. If you are upset about things at work – talk to people AT WORK about how to make improvements. Spend your energy coming up with ideas and solutions. Don't waste your precious time when you are *not* at work, complaining about work!

Eliminating talk of workloads at the Smith College dinner table was a great habit to start at a young age. You need to be able to talk

about more than just your work.

We had the same rule at a "dinner club" that my sister and I were part of. No *shop talk*. If anyone started drifting into tales of work minutia, everyone else would all start pretending to fall asleep. (All I can say is that we married guys in the group - so it must have been a pretty good rule!)

In Paris, I don't remember anyone asking me what I did for work. They asked me what I thought, what I was interested in and what I enjoyed. I loved that about Paris.

Having said that, it is important to find work that you love. You will need to experiment and be open to try new things. I have worked with lawyers, police deputies, engineers, young kids and CEOs. I have painted murals, run a non-profit gift company, designed computer games and more. Most of the jobs I had, I didn't even know existed – or I created them when I got to a company. I tapped into the things that I liked to do and found ways to help others meet their goals using my skills.

What do you love doing?

 **ACTION STEP**: Let's identify work that you *enjoy* doing and work you *don't enjoy*. Then you can look for ways to do more of what you like and less of what you don't.

What do you get lost in - when you forget to eat and stay up late to work on?

_____

_____

_____

_____

_____

When you have a great day at work, what are you doing?

_____

_____

_____

_____

_____

_____

_____

ACTION STEP: What are 5 things you love doing? What skills do you have? What are you good at? (Photography, meeting new people, spreadsheets, puzzles, sports, training dogs, singing, listening – it can be anything.)

TOP 5 THINGS THAT I LOVE/THAT I'M GOOD AT:

1)

2)

3)

4)

5)

3 THINGS THAT I DO *NOT* LIKE:

1)

2)

3)

ACTION STEP: Make a list of things that you would like to do more of at work and what you would like to do less of at work.

I WOULD LIKE TO DO *MORE*:   **I WOULD LIKE TO DO *LESS*:**

ACTION STEP: If you could create your own perfect job, what would that look like?

Would you work inside? Outside? Work at a company with thousands of people or a few employees? Would you work quietly on your own or would you want to manage and lead others? Salary range? Commute? Amount of travel? Type of people you'd work with? Kinds of things you are passionate about: computers, art, food, health, physical exercise, music...

Write the specifics of what your perfect job looks like.

_____

_____

_____

_____

_____

_____

_____

_____

_____

_____

_____

_____

_____

_____

_____

_____

_____

_____

_____

_____

Chapter 14

The journey, not the arrival, matters.

"Don't be too timid and squeamish about your actions.
All life is an experiment."
- RALPH WALDO EMERSON

It is easy to talk about experimenting and another thing to actually do it. Plus, it gets harder as you get older. You're rooted in your routines and habits. You forget about possibilities and trying new things. You get stuck. You stop the journey. You stop experimenting and learning. You stop LIVING your life. Here are some ways to start getting back on the journey.

Boston, November 2011

Can you do it without a cabin?

A hundred years ago, when I was single, I used to help one of my dear friends, Lisa every August 15th or so, with Medal Day at the MacDowell Colony in Peterborough, NH. (Lisa's family managed MacDowell.)

The MacDowell Colony is a retreat haven for distinguished artists that takes away all the noises and distractions in everyday life and allows these geniuses to focus on their art. The "Fellows" have a quiet cabin in the woods. No phones. Breakfast and dinner are prepared for them at the Main House and picnic basket lunches are quietly dropped off at their cabin door during the day.

Medal Day weekend is the only time during the year that MacDowell opens up its grounds to the public. They choose an incredible artist who has made significant contributions to his/her field – a different artistic discipline is selected each year. (Lisa and I were at MacDowell not as incredible artists – although of course we both are. We were there as waitstaff. Or hostesses. Or whatever other euphemism you prefer.)

Fond memories of these weekends include my nearly spilling hot tea on the president of NY's Lincoln Center and having an adjoining bathroom with the very funny and talented writer George Plimpton.

I also got to meet the astounding Leonard Bernstein – who was a medalist and MacDowell Fellow and I met the genius *Sophie's Choice* author, William Styron. They were amazing weekends.

But it has taken me all these years to realize what I had overlooked at the time: The value of the cabin.

Virginia Woolf said, *"A woman must have money and a room of her own if she is to write."*

How true!

I am writing a book. I love it! I would write all day and all night if I could. I fantasize about having my own cabin – although mine is by the ocean – to sit and actually get to write!

(It reminds me of a cooking class I took. We had an array of expensive, fresh ingredients, proper tools and lots of time to prepare. The better test for a great chef, if you ask me, is someone who can make a delicious meal - when there's only crackers, cucumbers and SpaghettiOs™ in the house - while tending to a crying, hungry child.)

The same goes for art. I have given myself a little "time" – which is fantastic but even with that, it is tough. I am a heads-down, pit bull kind of writer. I get in the "zone" and it is hard to start and stop. Which means having uninterrupted time. And unless you're a MacDowell Fellow in the backwoods of NH, I don't know how people do it.

How do you zone out from life to write, yet still be there to go over spelling words and get to the gym? How do you power down from email, phone calls and texts without having your friends and family disown you?

At some point I have to start making money, so this time is "extra precious" knowing that I won't always have this luxury. So I'm trying to write as fast as I can but I need my own space. I'm not talking about a cabin even, I'd settle for a set of headphones or a "Cone of Silence."

With all due respect to medalists Maestro Bernstein and Pulitzer-Prize winner Styron, I think the truly inspirational artists are the ones who find the time and space to create art *in the midst* of all of life's distractions. Perhaps MacDowell can have a special Medal Day category (The "No Cabin" medal) for artists who find a way to create *without a cabin*. Who knows, maybe even bad tea pourers can win!

Boston, December 2011

What if you won the lottery?

My husband bought me a Powerball ticket yesterday. The jackpot was $245 Million. I just checked my ticket. I didn't win.

It reminded me of a conversation I just had with someone who had been in his job for 10 years and was burned out. He wasn't happy but he didn't even know what to do – or where to start to make a change.

I asked him, "What would you do if you won the lottery? What if you couldn't fail? What if money were no object, what would you do?"

Most of us don't really know. It takes some exploration to find what you love – to remember what you love.

What made you smile and jump up and down as a kid? What do you love doing? When you have a great day, what does that look like? What were you doing? What do you get lost in – when you forget to eat and stay up late to work on?

These questions are a great place to start. (See the *Action Steps*.)

I am in that place now. I have won my own little lottery. My prize is time. I've given myself a little time to try and figure out what to do next. I'm writing a book. I'm blogging. I'm exploring creating a new education model. I'm exercising. I'm getting to be with my kids. I'm jumping out of bed in the morning. I'm thrilled with my winnings. What about you?

Boston, October 2011

Start anyway

I miss the show – *Studio 60 on the Sunset Strip* – starring Matthew Perry. It was a "behind the scenes" fictional Saturday Night Live show (except their show aired on Fridays). It was in *"The West Wing"* style and gave a glimpse of what it is really like (and the crazy pressure!) of producing a live television show.

One thing I remember was the big digital clock that ticked backwards in Matthew Perry's office to show him how many hours (minutes) he had each week until the show started. Ready or not, no matter what, their show went live at 11:30 p.m. Friday night. There's a good lesson in that.

I had a big meeting today. I got myself into a crazy spin yesterday not feeling ready. Not knowing what I was going to say.

My answer to that? I turned off the computer and took the kids trick-or-treating. Because guess what? You can plan all you want. You don't make ANY progress until you take action. Until you take a step. It's hard though, when you want things to be perfect, and you know they aren't, and you take a step anyway.

The only way that you make progress is to start. Even knowing that you don't have things exactly as you want them. Otherwise, you keep editing, changing, updating…and you'll NEVER be done. Having a deadline, meeting or TV show – is a great reminder that sometimes you have to start anyway, ready or not.

I can feel that with each meeting I'm getting a little bit better. Plus, I'm a lot further along than if I were just sitting and trying to make things perfect and never jumping in.

That's why software has numbers (e.g., version 3.6). They know it's not perfect but it's working and they'll get user feedback and make adjustments and then launch version 3.7.

It's what we need to do with our lives: Act. Assess. Adjust. *Repeat.*

Summary: Find work that you love

"I *would* do what I love – if I only knew what that was!"

There are so many options that it's easy to get overwhelmed. You don't know what to do, so you don't start. Or you just do whatever is easiest. Plus, there is the added pressure of having to support yourself – and perhaps others – so there are often trade-offs between what you love and what you need to do.

Take a deep breath. See the moments that are tugging at you. Pay attention to things that bring you joy. Believe in the possibilities. You *can* create a life that includes work that is fulfilling *and* provides the income you need, if you take an active role in creating your career. You have to *do* the work to *get* the work – put the energy into figuring out what makes you happy and start moving in that direction.

So, when exactly are you supposed to do all of this?

Our lives are jam-packed and the last thing you feel like doing is *more* work. The easy thing would be to do nothing. To give up before you start; to give in to the lizard brain. That is fine for other people but you are an *Action Hero* for your life. You just need to take a step.

Put on some great music, take a deep breath and imagine the possibilities of doing something you love. Commit to spending an hour this week (in a few 15-minute chunks) and taking small steps towards making change happen. Start by doing the *Action Steps*.

The *Action Steps* have you try something new each week and to be proud of the work you are doing – no matter how big or how small – and put your name on it; "sign it." You will start to identify what you get lost in, what you are good at and what kind of things you love. The *Action Steps* ask you to write down what makes you unique and for you to ask others to describe you. Take a look through your answers. These are clues to finding what you love and then finding jobs where you could use these things. You match what *you have* with what *companies need*. (Or perhaps, even start your own company.)

Let's say you are good at making people feel at ease. What kinds of places need people who can *make others feel at ease?* Think of places where people do *not* feel at ease: at hospitals; with technology; at college admissions offices. You could start your exploration with those types of environments. It may not be intuitive – which is why you need to experiment. Do online searches on some of the words you used to describe what you like doing and see what kind of jobs are listed. What kinds of companies need these skills?

I was an art and psychology major, who never took a computer class, and became a CIO. I used what I knew (design, understanding people, making people feel comfortable). I helped to make technology easy to use, from a design sense. I could understand what people wanted (user experience). I could explain complicated things in ways that aren't intimidating and put people at ease. I didn't "know" I was good at this. I had to experiment. I tried different jobs.

So how do YOU start experimenting?

Think of 5 companies you love and 5 people whom you admire and have fabulous jobs. Why do their jobs appeal to you? Do these jobs match your description of your perfect job from the *Action Steps?* If not, take some time to really think big – dream about what would make you happy. Why do you love these companies: their products, their mission, their culture? Start researching these and similar companies. Start talking to people. Tap into online career resources and social media sites to find people you know at these companies and what it's really like to work there. Ask for help. You can do this. You just need to believe in the possibility and take little steps.

Often you just need to get "in the door" of a good place; whether that be an internship, as a volunteer, part-time or in a role that may not be the *perfect* fit right now, but has good potential. Once you are working there, you can see firsthand what the company needs and work on creating a role for yourself. It's about taking an active role in your career - like my friend Andy did.

Andy loved sports. He spent hours watching games and keeping up on players, coaches and stats. He took a job as a receptionist at a sports TV station in Boston. He met people. (In fact, he met *everyone* who came through the door.) He paid attention. He "signed" his work, giving it his all on the little things. He didn't worry about a job that was "below" him. He saw it as an opportunity and had a great attitude.

He made a positive name for himself. When roles opened up, he applied for them. He eventually became Executive Producer of one of the biggest sports stations in Boston. One step at a time.

You may not even have to leave your company to find a better job. Perhaps you're at a good company but just need to make some changes to your role. We discussed asking for what you want, becoming a good negotiator and standing up for yourself and what you believe in.

What would you like to do more of (and less of)? Can you come up with a plan to present to your boss that makes sense for the company? The work that you don't like, still needs to get done. What about new possibilities? Does someone else love doing the work that you don't? Could you reshuffle the roles? Could you find a different way to get the work done? How could this benefit the company?

But, it is so easy to get overwhelmed and give up before you start.

"I'm just trying to make ends meet and don't want to rock the boat. Plus, I'm tired and it's tough. Who has the time? It's not *horrible*."

(*That's* how you want to live your life? 'It's not horrible?')

Remember, *you deserve to be happy*. You *can* live a BIG, fabulous life. You *can* find work that is fulfilling and provides income for you and your family. You spend so much of your life working. Why *not* make it something that you feel good about and that makes a difference? Why *not* do something that makes you happy; something that is better than "it's not horrible?"

I get that it's tough...and scary. Remember, I am doing this too. But there are SO many people, books, resources and sites devoted to helping you figure this out. The important thing is for you to take a step – any step – in the direction of finding work that you love. If you need more training or education for a better job, then you can start there. But you can do it – if you want it and are willing to do the work. It happens with little steps. You can do them in 15-minute chunks. Isn't your life worth that? Dedicating 15 minutes today? You can do that.

And you don't have to do it alone.

The next section talks about the importance of having supportive people in your life and building deep and trusting relationships.

Build strong
relationships

ଔ

Chapter 15

Treat everyone you meet with respect. Encourage them to astound you.

"If you treat an individual... as if he were what he ought to be and could be, he will become what he ought to be and could be."
– JOHANN WOLFGANG VON GOETHE

My first job as a college graduate was as a "temp." I was treated poorly and I never forgot it. No one expected anything from me and that's what they got. Here are some stories from the other side of that coin. People treating everyone they meet with respect – and the magic that can happen.

The gardener

My father-in-law was a great salesman. It wasn't what he did - it was who he was. He loved talking to people. He loved making connections. He loved helping people solve their problems.

He told me a story of early in his career when he had just left his company to go out on his own. It was risky to leave his steady paycheck but he believed in himself and the potential, and it was something he needed to try.

One of his first sales calls was at a big company. He drove up to the huge industrial park complex and noticed the beautiful flowers on the way in. He saw a gardener in old overalls working on the flowers and weeding the entranceway and my father-in-law struck up a conversation; telling the worker what a great job he was doing and how beautiful it all was.

The gardener thanked him and asked him who he was there to see. My father-in-law told him and the gardener said he would show him where that was. They walked in together and when they got to the company, my father-in-law was surprised at how many people this man knew. He was also surprised at his access. He was walking around as though he owned the place. Turned out, he did.

The gardener was the president of the company (who also enjoyed gardening). My father-in-law showed his true colors and was someone that the president wanted to do business with. He got this account and it was one of his major pieces of business for years to come.

Don't judge a book...

A friend of mine owned an expensive men's clothing store in Faneuil Hall in Boston. He told me a story of a grungy college student who came in one day and looked completely out of place in this high-end store – think Julia Roberts in *Pretty Woman*. The salesmen up front didn't pay much attention to him. My friend went right up to this young man and welcomed him and asked him how he could help him.

The student said that he needed a suit – for something the next day. The owner took great care of him and put a rush on the tailoring to get him what he needed. He treated him like a treasured customer.

The next week, a businessman came into the store looking for the owner. He said to my friend, "I wanted to thank you. My son came in here and needed a suit for a funeral and he told me how great you treated him. He had been to other stores and people weren't helping him. I need a few suits too." This man was extremely wealthy and he (and his friends) became big customers for my friend's store.

The power of nice

I heard a delightfully engaging woman speak in Boston, Linda Kaplan Thaler, who owns a large advertising agency in New York. Her book, *The Power of Nice*[7] talks about the experiences she had in advertising and many examples of the ripple effects of small actions of being nice.

One story she told us was about the filming of the TV show, *The Apprentice*, in its heyday, with Donald Trump. Her agency was selected as the advertising agency of choice for one of the big shows. Just before the cameras started rolling, Trump turned to her and said, "When my wife (Melania) was just starting out as a model, you were very good to her. She told me how you had fresh flowers in her trailer, helped her work through her nerves and made her feel comfortable. Thank you."

He then proceeded to tell millions of people that her agency, The Kaplan Thaler Group, was "the best advertising agency in New York City." Quite an endorsement.

Linda told us that she had just treated the future Mrs. Donald Trump as she would anyone. She was nice to her.

I got to see Linda's kindness firsthand when I contacted her, after hearing her speak, and she became a client of mine. She is the real deal. She sets a great example. The power of nice.

ACTION STEP: Thank as many people as you can today.

Thank someone for holding the door. Thank the bus driver. Thank your waitress. Thank your coach. Thank your teacher. Thank your spouse. Thank your kids. Thank a workman for creating good work. Tell them you appreciate what they are doing; that you appreciate their hard work. (Then do it again tomorrow with new people.) Be kind. Be nice.

Chapter 16

Find and nurture deep relationships.

"Let us be grateful to people who make us happy, they are the charming gardeners who make our souls blossom."

– MARCEL PROUST

It is often said, "It's not what you know, it's who you know." You MUST do the hard work, but it is just as important, if not more so, to also have strong relationships. Build up a trusted network. Do a lot of favors. Help others. Be someone people can count on. Show up when you say you will. Do what you say you will do.

Boston, 2002 - 2005

One of my bosses was a very connected, extremely high-energy CEO. She knew everyone. She was great with connecting people. Sharon Whiteley changed my life.

I worked with her for three years as her CIO. We had teams in Boston, San Francisco and India. We did a deal with Yahoo!. We struggled with typical startup issues – little money, long hours, difficult decisions. I worked mostly from home so I could be with my young children. I stayed on for longer than I had planned. I owed her. She had been so good to me – especially for the gift of "my sisters."

Newport, September 2004

My amazing *sisters*

I was invited to Newport, RI for some kind of retreat. I didn't know more than that but trusted Sharon when she told me I needed to go. So I went. Sharon had nominated me for a women's group – which was to be a new "feeder group" to an established group. A huge *moment* in my life!

The group was the female equivalent to The Bohemian Grove which is a secret, men's group – the "old boys network" where U.S. presidents, CEOs and prominent men get together, smoke cigars, make deals and help each other with access to capital, business issues, etc. Or so I have been told. Women are not allowed in.

A group of dynamic women wanted the same kind of group where women could help each other with their businesses and just let their hair down in a supportive environment. And they *took a step* – and started one with a few of their friends.

It blossomed into an amazing group of women – most of whom are in their 50s and 60s and have lead incredible lives. The weekend in Newport, RI was the first retreat for the *next generation* of the group. I am forever indebted to Susan Stautberg and Edie Weiner for their vision for starting this phenomenal group and for the incredible examples they set in helping women.

Each year we have a four-day retreat in a phenomenal place. We've been to Belize, Costa Rica, Ecuador, Colombia, the Dominican Republic and more. Typically, government officials and prominent business people meet with us and we try and help out the local community.

My first big retreat was in Costa Rica. There were only seven of us "newbies" and about 100 or so of the original group. On the plane I was reading the bios and was completely intimidated. These women were amazing! Executives at Fortune 500s. Ambassadors. Financial wizards. Government officials. Very, very, powerful women. What was I doing here? I am not worthy. How did I get in?

What I have learned is that it takes more than a resume. It's about kindness. It's about a sense of humor, adventure and spirit. It is truly a sisterhood. We care deeply about each other and about helping each other succeed. The women I have met over the past seven years are my dearest friends. My sisters.

The retreat is also brilliant in that there are **no** PowerPoint presentations. We don't sit inside in conference rooms. We have inspiring seminars in casual settings outside by the beach, followed by an afternoon adventure that could be snorkeling, zip lining or speaking at a local high school. We have amazing dinners, incredible connections and conversations. We get refreshed and rejuvenated.

To reassure you that I haven't lost my *"You're no fun anymore"* spirit: Every year I write a song and recruit that year's inductees to be my backup singers and dancers on stage – which usually involves wigs, boas and sequins – and we perform in front of about 200 or so of some of the most influential women in the world. *Year of Action!*

I invest a lot in these relationships. I help others. I get back so much more than I give. It is truly a highlight of my year – and one of the biggest gifts in my life. Thank you Sharon.

The power of friends

Do not underestimate the power of friends, especially your women friends. It doesn't have to be flying to Costa Rica either. It is just as important to meet for spur of the moment coffees or "Mommy and Me" classes. Some of my dearest friends are women I met at "Icky Sticky Goo" and "Tumblin' Twos" classes. Where, amid the finger paints and Legos™, I found incredible women and had wonderful laughs (and therapy sessions) with them.

ACTION STEP: We are all busy. You *can* make the time. Call someone you haven't seen in a while and meet for coffee or a quick walk – even for 20 minutes. It will be so worth it! Your relationships are precious and need to be nurtured.

Chapter 17

Small actions can have a big ripple effect.

"Life's most persistent and urgent question is...
what are you doing for others?"

- MARTIN LUTHER KING, JR.

In work and in life, you never know how these little moments will impact your life – or will impact others. Moments like these:

Boston, September 2011

Sliding doors

I love the movie *Sliding Doors* with Gwyneth Paltrow. The first scene shows Paltrow dashing down the stairs trying to catch the subway. A child gets in her way and the doors slide shut. She doesn't make the train. Then you see a replay of the same scene, but this time the child's father simply puts his hand out to gently block the child and now Paltrow makes the train.

The movie shows you her life from *both* versions and the dramatic difference from that seemingly nothing event, from that tiny *moment*.

We never know the impact things have or the ripple effect we have on others' lives. This fall was our 17th year walking *The Boston Marathon Jimmy Fund Walk*™ for the Dana-Farber Cancer Institute and it made me think of *Sliding Doors*.

After we had done the Jimmy Fund Walk for eight years, I felt like taking a break. It is a lot of work raising money, doing the training walks and soliciting your friends. Plus, it's the Boston Marathon – 26 miles! Besides, life is busy.

Then a *moment* happened.

I got a call that Andrew, one of my son's friends, had cancer. He was six. We can't quit now.

His type of cancer was called Neuroblastoma – which is a rare and extremely aggressive cancer. Since it is rare, there was little research dedicated to it.

It was the fall of 2004. The Red Sox had made it to the playoffs as the Wild Card team but had little hope of going to the Series. They were down 3-0 after an embarrassing 19-8 loss. All looked grim. Then the unbelievable happened. They came back to win four in a row – against the Yankees! Boston was crazy! My brother Jim called me on Friday after the game and asked me to do him a favor.

I said, "Sure."

"You don't even know what it is."

"Okay – what is it?"

"Will you take Mom and Dad to the World Series?"

"What!?"

My brothers had moved out of state years earlier and my sister and I were the ones who helped with the many doctor/hospital visits for my dad, who had more than his share of illnesses.

I said, "That is unbelievable! But ticket prices are out of control. I'll drive them to the game but you don't have to get me a ticket."

He said, "I'm getting four tickets – you, Maura (my sister), Mom and Dad. I want to thank you for all you have done for Mom and Dad."

Maura was eight months pregnant – and as much as she is a huge Red Sox fan – she wasn't thrilled about being jostled around in the hyped-up crowd.

She said, "You know, a while ago I asked Dad who his best friend was and he said, 'Uncle Ed.' What if we gave my ticket to Uncle Ed?"

Uncle Ed had just been diagnosed with brain cancer. He was going to be at Dana-Farber on Monday to review his options.

These brothers had been die-hard Red Sox fans all of their lives and had lived through more than 65 years of heartaches.

Sunday morning we did a conference call with Uncle Ed and asked him where he was going to watch the game that night. He said he was going to his son Paul's, who had a big TV.

We said, "We have an even better seat than that. How would you like to go to the game?"

It was an incredible night. It was the Curt Schilling bloody sock game. Dad and Uncle Ed (and Mom and I) saw our beloved Red Sox win! (My brother made us paint big Red Sox B's on our faces. He also made my mother hold up a sign that said, "I'm Curt Schilling's mother" and bring back pictures of it. There are no free lunches!)

Meanwhile, we were still fundraising for the Jimmy Fund Walk. I had talked to Dana-Farber about earmarking these funds directly to Neuroblastoma. They told me about a family in Needham that had been working on raising $1 million.

If we could get to $1 million, Dana-Farber could establish a Neuroblastoma Center that would ensure research for this rare cancer going forward.

The $1M goal for the Neuroblastoma Center was $10,000 short. Our "walk goal" was $10,000 and we were $800 short. Then an amazing *moment* happened.

We got an unexpected letter in the mail.

My cousin Ed - Uncle Ed's son - had won a sales contest at work for $800. He wanted to thank us for taking his father to the World Series – a priceless dream come true. He signed the check over to *The Jimmy Fund*. We made our $10,000. We sent it to the $1 million fund and they made their goal. There is now a Neuroblastoma Center at Dana-Farber, the only one in New England.

THIS PAST FALL, at mile 22 of *The Walk*, I sat down at a pit stop to tie my shoes. Someone sat down next to me to tie hers too. Her green shirt was emblazoned with a big *NB* on the front. She was part of a *huge* team of walkers.

I said, "NB. Is that Neuroblastoma?"

She said, "Yes."

I smiled. Then I saw the beautiful little girl who was being treated at the Neuroblastoma Center at Dana-Farber. Just then, the "T" (subway) went by at Cleveland Circle and the doors opened.

It is amazing how many lives are changed by people taking action on seemingly little moments. *These* are the real-life *Action Heroes*. Everyday people like you and me.

Boston, February 1992

The girl next door

My sister and I lived in a great apartment complex in Boston. We loved it. Then the landlord raised the rent by 20 percent. We couldn't afford the increase. We could barely afford it as it was. We had to move...in February. Who moves in February?

We had both just broken up with guys. It was the middle of winter. We had to move from a place we loved. I had just turned 30. No job. No love. No place to live. I was miserable.

Little did I know this was a great *moment* in my life.

There was limited inventory of apartments at this time of year. We ventured further away from the city and finally found a place. When I walked into the front room, I felt something special. Rays of sun shined brightly through the window and it felt like home. This was it!

My sister didn't get the same warm and fuzzy feeling I did. She had a more literal vision – that of an old apartment that had been vacant for months and filthy. There was food (well presumably it was food) still in the refrigerator and dead flies on the floor from having the windows open since July.

Through all of this, I could see the potential. It was in a great location in Newton Centre and it was available and affordable. We could fix it up. My sister wasn't biting. She would *never* live there.

She went to work the next day and her co-workers helped to convince her to reconsider. We had been looking and looking and this was the best place we had seen. We moved in.

Good thing too. As it turns out, I am the "girl next door." So is my sister. We married our neighbors.

It all started when we least expected.

One night, shortly after we had moved in, my sister and I were feeling sorry for ourselves. We were both just getting over breakups. We were still upset that we had to move out of a place we loved. And here we were on a rainy Friday night in our sweatpants and we didn't know anyone. I had just finished saying that we can't sit around waiting for someone to knock on our door, when someone knocked on our door. (Well actually, they rang the doorbell.)

It was our neighbor asking if we wanted to join them at a local bar. I ran back upstairs and said to my sister, "Get dressed. We're going out." So started our friendship with the guys next door, Matt and Bill.

Matt had started something called *CPC* (Clean Plate Club). It was a group of Boston College guys, none of whom really cooked. Matt thought it wasn't too much to ask, to have a decent meal one night a week. One guy would host and provide the main course and everyone else would bring something (appetizer, dessert, salad, drinks).

The motto was, "*Quantity and hopefully, Quality.*" It didn't matter *what* you cooked – as long as you made plenty of it. They invited us one night. I forgot what we were asked to bring. I do remember that they cooked a ham. I remember this because of the taunting I got repeatedly after that night.

During the meal I said, "Nice ham, Bob."

Then I cringed thinking, "Wait, what is his name?" Matt didn't let me get away with that.

"Did you just call him *Bob*?"

"Uh..."

My sister mouthed to me that his name was Bill.

Then everyone started saying, "Nice ham, BOB!"

We all started laughing. And with that, we were inducted in as full-fledged CPC members. The first women! (They hadn't discovered yet that we couldn't cook.)

Matt and I continued just as friends. In fact, I thought he liked my sister. Then he asked me out. (Love shows up when you least expect it.)

Boston, September 1992

Peggy

Matt is very close to his brother, Kelley. They were in business together and they spent a lot of time together outside of work too - along with Kelley's wife, Peggy. Peggy's avocation was trying to fix up Matt. She was happy when I appeared on the scene. The four of us became fast friends and spent a lot of time together. Kelley and Peggy had three young children.

Matt and I were supposed to have dinner one night and I got a message from him saying that Peggy had collapsed and was in the hospital. I didn't know much more than that. I wasn't worried though. She was young and healthy.

He called back. She died.

My knees gave out. What? How could she have died? I just talked with her yesterday. She was fine.

Somehow I drove to the hospital in a daze. When I walked in and saw Kelley it hit me, "Oh my God, the kids!"

Peggy had a brain aneurism and died. She was 31. It was all too much to believe. The beautiful kids – ages 3, 2 and 11 months old have lost their mother. No. This can't be happening.

Her funeral was one of the saddest days of my life.

It was during this incredibly sad time that I truly fell in love with my would-be husband. He was unbelievable. He jumped in and did everything – all under the radar. He was running the business solo. He took care of all the bills – both at work and at Kelley's house. He set up a weekly night where he said to Kelley, "I will be here every Wednesday night. Go out, take a nap, do whatever you want. You'll be off duty. I will be here and watch the kids."

I knew then that this was who I wanted to have in my life – who I wanted to go through life with. Someone who would make me laugh and be there on the tough Wednesday nights in my life – and every other night too. So in a way, Peggy really did bring us together.

Boston, December 1994

George Costanza

Shortly after we got married, we met up with some of my Spinnaker friends for brunch. Matt and I sat next to Nancy. Nancy and I had known each other over the years through the Spinnaker gang and she had just moved to Boston. She went on and on about how great she thought Matt was – more than the obligatory, "I am happy for you and your new husband."

I thought, *hmmm*, if she likes Matt, she would like his brother, Kelley, too.

I called Nancy and said, "I'm not sure how this works but I was thinking that you're new in Boston and I'd love to fix you up with Matt's brother, Kelley. I have to warn you, *on paper*, he may not seem that great...his wife died and he has three kids...but other than that he's an amazing guy."

Lucky for all of us, Nancy had been watching *Seinfeld*. Specifically, it was the episode where George Costanza does the exact opposite of what his instincts tell him to do. Nancy said that normally she wouldn't go on a blind date, but like George, she would do the opposite. She would go. (A variation on "Never say never.")

Boston, June 1996

17 lives

Nancy and Kelley were married about a year later.

It is amazing to think of all the lives that were affected by the one simple *moment* - the move into the Newton Centre apartment – which you may remember, we didn't want to do.

There were two guys across the hall, Matt and Bill. I married Matt and we had two kids. My sister married Bill, and they had three kids. I fixed up Matt's brother Kelley with my friend Nancy and they got married. His three kids gained a mother and they had another child.

Our other neighbor in the house was Alison. She was like a sister to us and more importantly, was also inducted into CPC. (After she made

Cornish Game Hens for her first meal though, we knew she was way out of our league.)

Alison met a fabulous guy, Rob. As things got serious, she got cold feet. This guy was wonderful and I let her know that she just needed to talk to him about her concerns. They were great together and I urged her not to sabotage this relationship. She listened. They got married - and my daughter was a flower girl at the wedding!

2+2+2+3+2+3+1+2. A huge ripple effect on 17 lives from that one small moment.

ACTION STEP: Do something today to help someone. Don't just ask, "Do you need any help?" People often won't tell you or are afraid to ask. Just act.

Show up with a dinner to someone having a hard time. Help someone write her resume. Take someone's kids for an afternoon. Don't expect something in return, just keep putting out good and helping others and the ripples will begin. It doesn't matter if you see the ripples or not – they are there.

ᙉ

Summary: Build strong relationships

When all is said and done, it's about people. It's about people you connect with and impact - both directly and indirectly - with your actions. It's about being kind to others, treating them with respect and encouraging them to astound you. It's about giving - with no strings attached and no expectations. Doing lots of favors. Helping as much as you can. No complaints or excuses.

The amazing thing is that when you live this way - giving and helping and being kind with no ulterior motive - it comes back to you. People *want* to return the favor. People want to help you. You are attracting goodness back into your life by putting it out there.

Make the time to build strong relationships.

ଓ

We have talked about how to follow your dreams, find work that you love and build strong relationships. We have given you some basic steps to take action. You have the start of your roadmap.

Even when you have the roadmap though, you can still get lost. You can be going along in your life, seeing the moments, believing in the possibilities and taking a step. You can be following the path to your BIG, fabulous life and you can get thrown off course.

The next section shows how you can get lost (and it will be the people in your life that help you find your way back).

Get lost

❦

Chapter 18

What am I doing?

"The trouble with not having a goal is that you can spend your life running up and down the field and never score."
- BILL COPELAND

There are times that you get so busy running around or just trying to keep your head above water, that you can lose sight of your life. Your life spins out of control. You stop seeing your "moments," stop believing in the possibilities and stop taking steps. You wonder how you got here and you don't know what to do. You get lost. This section is my journey of how I got lost.

Boston, May 2007

Forgot to get him off the bus

One thing I have learned is you are never done. You might get lulled into thinking that you have things figured out, but life is always changing. Add in children and let the juggling act begin.

Matt and I were both working outside the home and we had a crazy schedule of babysitters and Matt was doing part-time duty with his flexible schedule. This meant that he had to work on Saturdays so we only had Sunday together as a family. We had to cram everything into Sundays – chores, family time and normal life craziness. It seemed that life was just passing us by. We were always running around. The *"Sunday Night Blues"* would set in - the dread that it was all going to start up again. Then a *moment* happened.

One day, our babysitter "forgot" to get our son off the bus. FORGOT to get him off the bus?! That's it. What are we doing? What kind of life is this? We need to make some changes. We're not going to live like this anymore. Matt quit his job to stay at home with the kids.

This took some adjustments on all our parts. Matt was new to this. He hadn't made any of the doctor's appointments or done the laundry or been active with school. Plus he wasn't doing things the way *I* did.

I had to learn to let him do things *his* way. (This is worth repeating. I had to learn to let him do things *his* way – even if it was not *my* way.) Many women do not do this. They want their husbands to do things exactly like they do. Guess what? That's not going to happen. Just because it's different, it doesn't mean it's necessarily bad.

There are women who don't like the way their husbands do things and think that THEY (women) are the only ones who can do it. This is a mistake. Women have told me their husbands have never been home alone with the kids, never made dinner or never been to the grocery store. The husbands don't do it *right*. My advice is to *get over it*. Get out of the way. Learn to appreciate different and you may be surprised. (Or like me - ecstatic!)

AFTER THE FIRST year, we all settled into this new way of life. Once we figured it out, it was great. For example, Matt is a great cook. He puts the effort into making healthy meals. This is a huge job and something I never did well. When I used to put a big bowl of salad out with lettuce - and perhaps a tomato - no one ate it. Matt makes each of us our own salad with about 10 different ingredients – and we each only get the stuff that *we* love. Now the kids lick their bowls clean (sometimes literally) and are filled up on this so they don't eat as much of the unhealthy stuff later either.

Remember, "Never say never." It has been the best thing for our family for me to get out of the way and let Matt do his thing. He is unbelievably organized. He is active in the town, at church and keeps everything under control. He runs our family. It (he) is fantastic!

Boston, March 2007

A dream job

I found a perfect job. The woman who hired me was amazing and I loved working for her. On my first day she told me that it was as though I had just bought a company. Here was my budget. Go. It was a dream job. I was running an Innovation Group. I was thrilled. It was just what I wanted. Besides loving what I was doing, I had a flexible schedule, incredible benefits and an easy commute.

Everything was working beautifully. Then a *moment* happened.

The organization brought in a new president along with a number of new executives. The environment dramatically changed from one of possibility to one of fear. People were heads down. My boss left.

I had a successful, thriving group. We had built the fastest-growing program within the organization. I was meeting with top organizations from around the world that wanted to work with us. We were about the future. We were well respected and sought out. They even did an article on my group likening me to the Wizard of Oz and saying we were the group "behind the curtain" that made everyone look good.

I figured that regardless of all the tough changes that were going on around us, we were safe. We were producing good work. *If it ain't broke – don't fix it!*

I was wrong.

After my boss left, I became kind of an employee nomad. They didn't know what to do with me. I had four bosses in four years. My group was working to transform a stagnant industry. Not an easy task. To many, we represented the pain and fear associated with change. It was no picnic for anyone at the top to support us.

It became very stressful. They bounced us around and each boss had his own agenda. I felt like Sisyphus, endlessly pushing the rock up the hill, only to have it fall back down and having to start over.

This had been a dream job for me and I thought I could figure a way back. My finances were still being rebuilt from *Henry's Hearts* and we were living on one salary. I wasn't in a position to leave. Plus, it was good for the kids to have my husband at home and to have the great benefits from my job. I had survived bombs going off in Europe, Ted's fist-pounding sessions and having only two stamps to my name – surely I could figure this out. I kept trying. I ignored the *moments*.

Boston, December 2009

What am I doing?

The stress had gotten so bad that I ended up in the Emergency Room with a migraine, throwing up, with an IV hooked to my arm and I thought, "What am I doing?"

My husband saw this *moment* loud and clear – saying that nothing is worth this. And STILL, I stayed. I thought I could make it work.

Why didn't I just leave?

When I look back now it was actually amazing – if it weren't so upsetting – to think of what happened so quickly. Here I was a confident and talented woman with a string of successes and within a matter of months, I had been beaten down and had lost my confidence. It was as if my *Year of Action* had never happened. I had let a few people get to me – and I started to believe them when they said I was no good.

How did this happen?

It can happen very subtly - in small ways; in ways you want to brush off or overlook. I was in love with my work. It was not only a great job, but it was a perfect fit for my family. There were so many fabulous people. I couldn't believe that a few bad apples could ruin everything.

But they did. With each episode, a little bit of my self-confidence was being chipped away. And at some point, I started to believe it. I started to believe that I couldn't leave – and that if I did I would be running away in fear; defeated.

I kept trying to get back to the job I loved. I wanted to believe that was possible. That if I just tried harder or differently I could find it.

It is so easy from the outside looking in when you talk about change. Why don't women just leave abusive environments? Why do spouses stay with alcoholics? Why don't you just leave? I learned that it is not so easy when you are in the middle of it.

Psychologist Martin Seligman[8] coined the term, *Learned Helplessness,* in which scientists did a series of tests where they put dogs in cages and inflicted pain on them. The dogs got so used to being hurt without being able to do anything, that even *after* the cage doors were opened, the dogs didn't leave. They stayed and continued to get shocked. They learned they were helpless. They had given up.

As I sit here and write these words, it brings tears to my eyes. How can this be me? Why didn't I just leave? Why did I put up with this for so long?

Perhaps it was so that I could write this book and allow you to see this *moment* – see what you are going through and let you know that the cage door is open. That you can get out. That you need to see the moments, believe in the possibilities and take a step.

I finally did.

 **ACTION STEP**: When your battery is worn down, it is hard to see the moments, hard to believe in the possibilities and hard to take a step. Yet, this is precisely what you need to do. Please listen to me when I say that, "It can be better. It will be better."

Do whatever you can to connect with others who can help you see your moments and to help you recharge your battery. You need to find the energy to be able to take a little step – and perhaps, prepare you for a big leap.

Chapter 19

Life, as you know it, can change in an instant. You can't take anything for granted.

"You will never find time for anything.
If you want time you must make it."
– CHARLES BUXTON

This chapter is a reminder that you can't wait. You can't keep postponing your life for "someday." You never know what is going to happen. Life can change in an instant. You need to start living it...today. Carpe Diem. Seize the day.

At the same time as all the stress and changes were going on at work, there were also some devastating things happening in my personal life.

May 31, 2009

Matt's father had been sick for a few years and was in assisted living. Matt was great. My work situation allowed him the opportunity to be there for his father. Matt would get the kids off to school, go down to his father's (about an hour away), get him outside in his wheelchair on a nice day, bring him the paper and have lunch with him. Then he would rush home and get the kids off the bus. His dad was getting worse and worse and it was getting near the end.

It was a Sunday and we were at my daughter's soccer game. Matt had a feeling that his father was going to die that day. More than any cosmic message, his thought was that his father was so "frugal" that he would want to get his full money's worth and die at the *end* of the month. You pay in advance for the nursing home – a month at a time – and Matt figured his dad would be so mad if his family had to pay for a full *month* if he died in the first few days of the month. No, Matt said his father would want to die at the end of the month. It was May 31st.

After Matt finished telling me this, his cell phone rang. It was his sister telling him that his father had died. Just then my daughter scored her first goal - ever. She had been playing for years and had never gotten a goal before. With that, Matt looked at me and said, "An angel gets his wings." She got her first goal with an assist from her grandfather.

September 22, 2009

We had just built a video studio at work and were having a big Hollywood, red carpet party for the opening. Our president was on hand to help us cut the ribbon and my team had invited their families. It had been a real labor of love to get this off the ground.

My husband and kids came. My parents came and got to see me in action and meet my whole staff. They were impressed that the president was there for my opening. They told me how proud they were of me. We all went out for dinner after the opening. It was a great night.

It was the last time I saw my father.

October 2, 2009

Don't wait

I had started calling my parents on my ride home from work. I would just do a quick 5 or 10-minute check-in. It seems that this became a welcomed ritual and something I had done a few hundred times or so. Yet on Thursday night, Oct 1st, I almost didn't call home. A move I would have regretted all of my life.

I had worked late. I was tired. I thought, "I'll just call them tomorrow."

For some reason, I called anyway.

I was telling my father a story that involved my daughter Lily – who by the way, was named after his mother, Lillian. When I got home Lily was still up and I had her finish the story directly with Papa. I could hear him laughing on the other end of the line even though I wasn't on the phone. She was cracking him up. She said, "I love you Papa" and we hung up.

The next morning I got a call from my mother. My dad had died in his sleep.

I got the call at work. I was in shock. I walked out of my office in a daze and I didn't know what to do. I just said, "My dad died" and burst into tears. I mumbled something about driving out to Worcester. I will never, ever, forget what happened then.

One of my staff, Marlene, dropped everything and said, "I'm driving you." (An hour away.)

Then another staff member, Kristen, said, "I'll follow you Marlene so you can get back."

They drove me straight to the hospital where my mom was all alone. My staff and colleagues sent food and flowers, came to the wake, sent cards and donations and came to the funeral. They had all just met my parents. My team and colleagues were spectacular.

October 2, 2009

The day he died

I was at my mom's house answering all the condolence calls, organ donor calls and making funeral arrangements. When during all the madness and chaos, I saw *my* doctor's name come up on my cell phone. I had made a follow-up appointment earlier in the week and figured they were just trying to reschedule it. I ignored the call. They called back and this time I answered it. It was the doctor himself. 5 p.m. on a Friday night and it was the doctor calling? This can't be good.

He said, "We retested your biopsy and we found cancer."

"Okay… Is that it?"

"This is serious. You need to come in right away."

"Not today I don't. I'll call you next week."

THE REASON THEY even discovered the cancer was incredible.

I was sitting in church (one of the few times in life when things are quiet and I can take a breath) and I felt a kind of tingling in my face and wondered if something might be wrong. It is probably nothing. After Mass, the kids were tugging on me to go to the church gym for donuts and I was on my way out with them when I saw a woman – I don't even know her name. We've said, "Hello" to each other a few times. She is an older woman and I know that her husband died and that she is alone. She always has a big smile.

At first I thought I would just wave from afar but something told me to go over to her. When I asked her how she was doing, she told me that she had melanoma and pointed on *her* face (to the EXACT spot that I had felt tingling on *my* face). I kind of looked up to the heavens and thought, "Okay, I hear you" and I called the doctor the next day.

I don't think I would have called the doctor had I not spoken to her. You couldn't see anything. I didn't have a mark or any outward sign that there was cancer.

I have never seen her since. I often wonder if she was some kind of angel.

When I saw the doctor I told him that I felt tingling and showed him where he needed to check. He told me that I wouldn't feel tingling. I persisted. They did a biopsy and the results came back negative. I wanted to be relieved but I could still feel something. I made a follow up appointment for a few months. That was Wednesday. There was no reason to retest my results.

My dad died on Friday. For some unknown reason they retested my results. They found my cancer the day my dad died. My uncle also found out that he had cancer that day too. (We are both fine.) I wonder if my dad had something to do with all of this.

I think that there are things right in front of us that we don't always see. There are messages that we don't always hear. Or choose not to. My scar is a reminder to not miss the signs that are all around me and to start to look at life a little differently – even if you have to look through bandages with black eyes.

Boston, February 2011

Life by the cup

This Saturday, I am at my kitchen counter with a cup of coffee looking out at four feet of snow and getting ready to go to my son's basketball game.

Last Saturday, I was having coffee by the pool in Cartagena, Colombia writing lyrics to a song I would be performing that night.

The Saturday before last, I was having coffee with my husband when we learned that his mother has stage 4 - lung cancer.

Three Saturdays. Three coffees. Three worlds.

Life…by the cup.

 **ACTION STEP**: Call someone you haven't spoken to in a while. Tell those you love how you feel. Don't wait. Imagine that this is the last day you will see everyone you meet today. How would you treat them?

Get found

☙

Chapter 20

Choose joy.

"Joy is not in things, it is in us."
– BENJAMIN FRANKLIN

Once you get lost, how do you get found? How do you dig yourself out from the hole you're in? Where do you even find the energy to start digging? This chapter shows how I climbed out of my hole and started to find my way back.

2009-2011

*I*n a very short period of time, there was a lot of stress, sadness and sickness in my life. It would be easy to fall into what Ben Zander[9] calls the "downward spiral," - talk that is based on fear and a resigned way of speaking that excludes possibility. Whatever you focus on will multiply. If you focus on the problems they will keep appearing. If you focus on the possibility, they will appear.

Work was awful with layoffs, many changes and a lot of stress. My father-in-law died. My mother-in-law died. My father died. On the day my dad died, I found out that I had cancer. I started to find my way back and out of the downward spiral after a few unlikely *moments* with some fish, some water, a face reader and a Little League game.

Boston, June 2011

Something fishy is going on

A watercolor fish mysteriously appeared on my kitchen island. After crack detective work, I discovered that my son had put it there. He had painted it years earlier and for no real reason he just brought it downstairs to make room for his Red Sox banner.

For no other reason than thinking we would be spilling juice on it any second, I went downstairs and pulled out an old frame. The picture fit beautifully. I robotically grabbed a hammer and nail and proceeded to hang it in our upstairs bathroom. I also hung up a ceramic fish – that my daughter had painted at least two years ago – that was buried in a pile of magazines on the floor and patiently waiting for someone to notice.

Ahhhh. That felt good. And looked good.

Then it hit me. This was how my *Year of Action* started. 25 years ago! I needed to get that feeling back.

I had been struggling lately. It was all I could do to just stay on top of things with mouths to feed and a mortgage to pay and being a mom – and missing important people in my life.

I felt like I was just going through the motions. I haven't been writing...or playing the piano...or meeting friends for coffee...or going out with my husband. I've lost my *Year of Action* rhythm.

And although it seemed like those fish appeared for no real reason,

 I think they were trying to tell me something. You have to keep moving (especially them or they die).

It is time to dust things off, get up and get going. Start fist pumping again. *Year of Action!* Start taking little steps back until I find my rhythm. Start feeling alive again. Find the joy.

Strafford, July 2011

Wipe Out

One of the worst shows you'll love watching is *Wipe Out*. It is ridiculous. Contestants try to jump across obstacle courses on rafts before getting knocked into the water by a huge 25-foot blow-up hammer. You can't help but laugh.

Last weekend we were in Strafford, VT with three other families. It is a beautiful little town of 1,300 people near the New Hampshire border. Our friends have a wonderful place with their own "swimming hole." As we drove up their hill, we saw it. Actually, my 12-year-old son saw it and said, "*Awesome!*" It was our own version of *Wipe Out.*

There in the middle of the pond, was a 15-foot raft, with a rolling-log type obstacle course and a trampoline top. The kids had their suits on in minutes.

Soon the chanting started, *"Wipe Out! Wipe Out!"* and a brave 10-year-old would stand up, run across the trampoline raft and jump onto the spinning log. If you're lucky, you can make a few steps before you go flailing into the water. It doesn't get any better than this.

Swimming's not my thing. I *can* swim. I'm just not very good. So the thought of just making it out to the raft, made me a little nervous. Yet, I knew I had to do it. I don't want to be one of those old ladies who never goes in the water or doesn't want to get her hair wet.

Once you reach the raft, you have to pull yourself up onto the platform. (Imagine a seal at the aquarium who does a belly slide up onto the deck at feeding time to applause.) Yet, trust me, there was no applause for my maneuver. Then you hoist yourself up on the trampoline raft. *Ahhhh*. I made it. But wait. That was the easy part.

Surprisingly, two more moms, Monica and Wendy, joined me up on the raft and we did a kind of adult *Ring Around the Rosy* – minus the singing and with a lot more falling down and hysterical laughing – the kind where you can't catch your breath, laughing.

Then the pack of kids and dads saw us and started chanting, *"Wipe Out! Wipe Out!"* A strange calm came over me. Perhaps it was the hyperventilating from the "Rosy circle" fits of laughter. Perhaps it was not letting myself think too much. Perhaps it was just time to have some fun.

I made it a respectable two steps on the spinning log before hitting the water. I have a newfound appreciation for the show contestants – my compatriots – and don't know how they do it!

What I do know is that my son came running up to me saying he couldn't believe I did it! He didn't go so far as saying he was proud of me or anything, but he did smile, which is prize money enough for me!

 **ACTION STEP**: When was the last time you were falling down laughing? Jump in and try something you think you're too old, too clumsy, too whatever to do. It feels great! Get wet. Have some fun! Get off the sidelines and jump in.

Cambridge, March 2011

I have big ears

I have big ears. Turns out that's a good thing. People with big ears are risk takers and leaders – who knew?

Patrician McCarthy for one. She is an amazing woman who for 20+ years has studied the art and science of Mien Shiang[10], a 3,000-year-old Taoist practice that literally means face *(mien)* reading *(shiang)*. She tells a story of how it saved her life. She was married to a doctor, yet it was a Mien Shiang expert she was interviewing for her thesis who saw in her face that she had an inflammation of the heart and convinced her to rush to the hospital right then for treatment. If she hadn't listened, it would have killed her.

I had the great privilege of attending a small workshop given by Patrician. I didn't know what to expect and, truth be told, wasn't expecting much. *Face Reading???*

It was life changing.

She "read" each of our faces in the "hot seat" in front of the group. She has a great perspective on melding Eastern and Western medicine.

Sometimes a pill is the best treatment and sometimes the learnings from 3,000-year-old Eastern practices are best.

She can tell about your childhood by looking at your ears. Your right ear is ages 1-7 and left is 8 -14. Things that happen in your life – both good and bad – show themselves through your body.

We could see portions of people's faces go shades of white, blue or yellow when she asked certain questions. She explained how to communicate with people (and deal with different kinds of people at work) depending on the shape of their face; their characteristics and tendencies. It was amazing.

The right side of your face is the mother, left is father. She could see grief lines on my father's side. I had cancer on my left cheek. She asked me if something had happened to me at work – changes in the structure, the authority? I told her that there were a lot of changes with the new management at work and I had lost my authority.

"I thought so. Your cheeks are your authority."

She could also see that my creativity was being stifled – crushed, really. Which for me, she could tell, is part of who I am. It is not a choice – it is just part of me and needs to get out.

My *moment* with Patrician was when she took hold of my arm and gently but emphatically whispered, "Listen to me. You need to make some changes. This is killing you."

It is impossible for me to do Patrician or her practice justice in trying to explain it with what little I know.

What I do know is that she was right. My life was killing me and I needed to make some changes. Luckily, with my big ears, I heard this *moment* loud and clear.

Boston, Spring 2011

Sometimes you make the catch

My son Jack was striking out much more than he'd been on base. In fact, he often was at the bottom of the lineup as well…and I couldn't be more proud of him.

One of the things I'm most proud of is that he has never once lost his temper, thrown his helmet, banged the bat against the chain link fence, or sulked or cried in the dugout. I bring this up because EVERY game, at least one of his young teammates does.

The pressure these kids put on themselves – or their parents put on them – is too much. These are 10, 11 and 12-year-olds. They're supposed to be having fun. Learning about sportsmanship. Learning the basics. Cheering on their teammates. Don't get me wrong. Jack LOVES baseball and he LOVES to win. But you can do it without slamming helmets and crying. *"There's no crying in baseball."*

Plus, then they get down on themselves. Lose their confidence. Drop the ball. Make a bad throw. It's a self-fulfilling prophecy. We could all learn a few things from young Jack and his recent game.

He was batting near the bottom of the order and struck out his first time up. The second time up he had a small hit just past the pitcher. He ran as hard as he could down to first base and got thrown out. No sulking. No fussing.

Then Jack's team took the field. It was the bottom of the 6th. (Only 6 innings in Little League.) There were a couple of errors on Jack's team and the other team started closing in. It was now 5-4. The tying run was on first and one of the best hitters was up. There were two outs. The batter hit a deep fly ball way out in Center Field. It was hit so high it seemed to hang in the air forever.

I held my breath. Jack was in Center and running back, back, back.

I felt like I was watching in slow motion as the ball came down – right into his glove! He caught the ball and they won the game!

It made me realize that even when it seems like you're always striking out and dropping the ball - sometimes you make the catch!

Life is about how you conduct yourself
between catches.

Cape Cod, Summer 2007 - 2011

The Brown Owl

I found an amazing beach house. It was a landmark in World War II and naval ships dubbed it *The Brown Owl* because its eaves made it look like an owl's eyes and the offshore buoy sounded like it was hooting.

We just called it paradise.

It is high up on a bluff on a private beach. I originally got the house when I needed a place for a last minute family gathering. My brother Jim and his family were going to be in Boston, my sister was on the Cape and my parents were in Worcester. I wanted an easy place for us all to get to – and I wanted it *on* the water.

We have been going to *The Brown Owl* ever since. It is before the Cape Cod bridge so there is no traffic. It can sleep 12 at least. Each summer we would have about 40 or 50 visitors during our stay and it never felt like we had any. It was such a joy to be able to share it and it made it more fun for us.

This year was the last year for *The Brown Owl*. The owners were retiring and they were going to move down there full-time. In fact, we learned that they were going to tear it down and rebuild it. So it's truly the end of an era.

Since this was going to be the last summer, we splurged and rented the house for *three* weeks - an extravagance that helped to change my life. My hope was that I could use that time to take a deep breath and figure out what to do about work. I had been through so much with sadness and stress and needed to just get away from it all. (There is also very limited, nearly non-existent, cell service - which makes it even better if you want to get away!)

ACTION STEP: Take a break. It's not a luxury – it's a necessity. It's like putting on your oxygen mask first before you can help others. You need to relax, recharge and rejuvenate. Take deep breaths. Choose joy. Laugh. You need to stop and not miss out on your life. Starting today.

You can take a little break right now. Close your eyes and take three long, slow breaths. Call in *well* one day to work – you're *well* enough to know you need a day off. Take a personal day. Take a Saturday or Sunday for yourself. Do something that brings you joy. It could be a long walk. It could be reading a book. It could be taking a free trial yoga class. You could go jump in a lake. Anything. Think of what would bring a smile to your face, and go do it. No excuses. *Year of Action!*

Chapter 21

Regain momentum.

"I know God will not give me anything I can't handle.
I just wish that He didn't trust me so much."
– MOTHER TERESA

Action is about movement and motion. The Year of Action is about taking a step and then another one. This chapter shows how you have to continue taking steps to regain your momentum. It's not just about starting to dig yourself out. You have to keep going forward so you don't slip back in the hole.

Cape Cod, Summer 2011

Life's simple pleasures

I was doing paperwork and paying bills and thinking how tough it would be to leave my job, when I came across a picture – a *moment* that reminded me not to take it all too seriously. It reminds me how lucky I am.

Usually, we're a family of four, but for the last seven years we have had a third child, Darion, from the Fresh Air Fund[11] during the summer.

It's a great experience for all of us.

During the year, when he's back in Harlem, we still feel his presence. We'll routinely say things like, "Put it on Darion's bed" throughout the year.

He's part of the family.

Over the years, we have done so many great things with him: Red Sox games, Newport, Cape Cod, lobster, parks, swimming, biking, mini-golf, camping – you name it, we've done it.

One night I asked him, "Of all the things that we've done, what are your top three favorites?"

He said, "Blueberry picking, baseball in the front yard and make your own pizza."

Pretty simple. Pretty telling. Life's simple pleasures.

It's a good reminder to do what you need to do to make sure you don't miss these *moments*. Even if it means staring down a pile of bills and taking a deep breath.

Boston, July 2011

Put it out there

"Once you make a decision, the universe conspires to make it happen."
– RALPH WALDO EMERSON

The book *The Secret*[12] was a huge success a few years ago. The premise is that if you put what you want out into the universe, the universe delivers. It's the *Law of Attraction*. Everything that is coming into your life, YOU are attracting. You attract what you are thinking. Therefore, if you want things to change, just change your thinking and believe it will happen.

That all sounds good – but when you're in the middle of a swirling life, often it's hard to find the strength to change your thinking. Plus, really? That's it? Change your thinking? Then a *moment* happened.

We went away for the weekend with friends and I took some time for myself and wrote in my journal. I wrote down what I wanted to do; things I wanted to happen. I saw them happening in my mind. I started believing that they were going to happen. At breakfast the next day with everyone, I said them out loud.

I got back to work and someone I hadn't seen in months, who I was thinking about over the weekend as someone who could help me, showed up at my door. I hadn't reached out to her – she came to me. We had breakfast the next day and the positive energy was contagious. She loved the changes I was talking about and wanted me to connect with two other people. Before I could reach out to them, one called me that day out of the blue. (I hadn't spoken with her in months.) And I bumped into the other one in the hall outside my office.

Then Thursday night I met up with some of my "sisters" for dinner. I told them what I was thinking. They were hugely supportive and I knew they would help me as needed too.

Driving home from the restaurant, I noticed that I was absent-mindedly humming a song. Then I realized that it was the song that my Dad and I had danced to at my wedding. It made me teary-eyed thinking maybe he was behind this.

I know that all of this may sound crazy – but I'm seeing it happen. The Universe presents what you need. It sounds nuts. All I know is that it's working, for a universe of one.

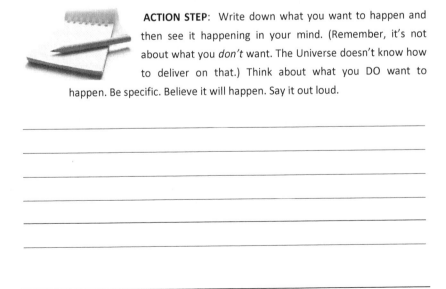

ACTION STEP: Write down what you want to happen and then see it happening in your mind. (Remember, it's not about what you *don't* want. The Universe doesn't know how to deliver on that.) Think about what you DO want to happen. Be specific. Believe it will happen. Say it out loud.

Yes Woman

We watched a movie the other night, *Yes Man*, starring Jim Carrey. It's about a guy who has given up on life. His wife left him. He spends his day as a junior loan officer denying loans for people. He never leaves his apartment. He never does anything. His friends are ready to disown him.

He bumps into an old friend who talks about a seminar, *Say Yes to Life*. He reluctantly goes with his friend to the seminar and agrees to say YES to EVERYTHING. He can't say "no" or the universe will conspire against him. He gives a homeless man a ride out to the woods, gives him his phone and his money. Gives out loans to everyone who comes into the bank. Learns to speak Korean, play the guitar and fly a plane. He meets the love of his life. It nearly all backfires though when his new love thinks he has been a fraud for not really *wanting* to do these things.

He modifies the Yes Philosophy and sees that sometimes you can say "no" but the main, knee-jerk response should be "yes". You need to WANT to do these things.

It reminds me of a poster that was in our pediatrician's office that started out with "Say yes as much as possible."

Do you want to play catch? Can we go to the playground? Can we have dessert first? Do you want to have a tea party? Can I invite a friend over? Do you want to color?

YES.

It's *not* about over committing. Women are often told they can't say no to people and end up being stressed and overworked. It's not that.

It's about saying yes to what's important to you, to what allows you to really live. And saying no to what's not important.

It's not always easy to say yes. We have "To Do" lists and responsibilities. We run around. But, you don't get this time back. When your knee-jerk reaction is no, you miss out on so much in life.

You don't regret what you try in life – even if you fall on your face. But you will regret NOT trying, not doing, not embracing, not helping and not believing in yourself.

 **ACTION STEP**: This week, say YES to one thing where you would usually say NO. And stand up for yourself and say NO to one thing where you are afraid to say NO.

Boston, Fall 2010

No waiting

We went away for the long weekend to a beautiful place on Cape Cod–along with about 200 other families who had the same idea we did. We all converged upon the only restaurant - a small pub-style place - at the same time. The kids were tired and hungry and it was crazy waiting for a table. I'm usually pretty patient but this made me nuts. It was so inefficient and poorly run and I realized…I hate to wait!

So – why do we wait on the important stuff?

We wait on life. I'll do it later. Someday. I'll go next year. I'll call him tomorrow. I'll go back to school when my life calms down. Not now kids – I'm busy.

We can't wait! Someday might not come. In fact, I'd guess it hardly ever comes. Someday needs to be now.

That's why when my son said last week when I got home late, "I wish we could go to the Science Museum."

I said, "Let's go tomorrow."

And we did.

It is why I was just at Shaw's supermarket buying cupcakes and balloons for Rufus' birthday party. (Rufus is my daughter's stuffed animal.) My daughter made invitations, invited a friend to sleep over, we sang "Happy Birthday," she passed out cupcakes to her other stuffed animals and she had a ball. I could have said, "Not now honey, let's wait."

But who likes to wait? What are you waiting for?

What are you waiting for?

Someday. Some other day that is not today. Some magic day when things happen. I am waiting for permission. I am waiting for someone to tell me that I can do it; to give me a little push; to tell me that it is not crazy. I am waiting for someone to believe in me.

I have learned that instead of waiting for someone else to give you permission or for someone else to believe in you, what if YOU gave yourself permission? What if YOU believed in yourself?

What are you waiting for?

_____

_____

_____

_____

_____

_____

_____

_____

ACTION STEP: Next time someone says, "We should have lunch" pull out your calendar right then and pick a date. When you have a weekend night with nothing to do – call friends and say, "Come on over for pizza." Take action and make plans the moment you talk about it. Don't wait.

Chapter 22

Do you want to live a big life?

"There is no passion to be found playing small - in settling for a life that is less than the one you are capable of living."

– NELSON MANDELA

We all want to be thought of; to be appreciated, to be missed. This means thinking beyond yourself and just your needs. It is about the bigger picture. What have you done for others? How have you contributed? Are you making a difference in someone else's life? Have you done work that matters? Have you helped someone? Are you living a big life?

Boston, April 2011

I was at a talk last night called *Women and Philanthropy*. Truth be told, I went because I knew one of the panelists, Diane Hessan, and wanted to see and support her – not because I wanted to give more. As is typically the case, when you do something for someone else, you get even more back. I was so inspired by the women in the room.

I learned that Diane became even more active *after* she had kids – partly to set a good example for her daughters. She used to tell them, *"You can choose to live a small life or a big life."*

I was surprised to learn that I'm the largest demographic of givers. Full-time working mothers! As I started to think about the Boards I am on and the groups that I am involved with, I surprised myself. I have no idea how I have found the time. I just did.

As I was writing my Dad's eulogy, it was abundantly clear that he lead a big life. It makes you stop and think about what you will look back on from your own life.

Saying you're busy these days is like saying you're *breathing*. We're all busy. It's not a contest to see who has the longest list. It's about what kind of life do you want to lead.

Giving needs to be a way of life. You just do it and you figure it out. It ebbs and flows. But don't complain about how busy you are! You can lead a big life in big ways and lots of small ways. It may take a little juggling but it's so worth it. And you can start today!

ACTION STEP: How is the world better by your being in it? What have you contributed? When was the last time you gave of your time for someone else?

Boston, July 1996

Visit from Peggy

I was up late. Very late. Matt had already gone to bed. For some strange reason something was keeping me up. I had to get up early for work and I wondered why I was staying up. There was no particular reason. I wasn't really watching TV or in the middle of a great book. I just was staying up. Finally, I went upstairs to go to bed.

1:15 a.m.

I had just gotten into bed and looked at the clock. 1:15? Why did I stay up so late? And just then an amazing *moment* happened. I had a conversation with Peggy. (Kelley's wife who had died.)

I didn't see her. I could feel her presence. It wasn't scary. It was very peaceful. I told her that the kids were doing great. I told her that Kelley had met someone and everybody was fine. All was okay. It made me feel very happy and calm and at peace.

The next night we happened to be at Kelley and Nancy's house for dinner. I was sitting next to Kelley and I said, "I'm not sure if you want to hear this – but I kind of had a conversation with Peggy last night."

"What time?"

"Actually, I know exactly what time. It was 1:15."

"She was around last night."

Peggy's sister Aimee was expecting her first child. She had gone into labor and was having a terrible time. The baby was 10 pounds and it was a very tough delivery. Kelley was on his way to the hospital and as he was driving in, he had a conversation with Peggy – at 1:15. And Aimee delivered a healthy baby boy - at 1:15.

THIS IS A very powerful *moment* in my life. If I was reading it I don't know if I would believe it. People may think that I was dreaming or that I imagined it or any other very reasonable sounding explanation. It is what I would be thinking. But I was there. I wasn't asleep. It happened and there isn't a reasonable explanation.

And just like the car that should have hit me but didn't when the guy ran the stop sign, the woman I met in church with the melanoma whom I have never seen again, the doctor retesting my results without any reason and discovered that I had cancer on the day my father died, the room and Henry heating up before his surgery, and now my conversation with Peggy – there are *moments* that happen that we can't explain.

All I can say is that I have a peace when I think about these moments. I think there are things bigger than us that we can't explain – so I don't try to. I am just open to life's moments. I have learned to look and listen for them. I physically get goose bumps now when I act on them. Something is going on. It makes me know that we are more than just ourselves. I don't try to figure it out or get freaked out – I am looking, listening and acting and each time I do, it all works out.

Chapter 23

Sometimes you need to take a leap of faith.

"And the day came when the risk to remain tight in a bud was more painful than the risk it took to blossom."

– ANAIS NIN

Every once in a while, you may have to leap. I hadn't really planned on leaping and I was doing all that I could not to leap. But sometimes, it becomes harder to stay put than to jump. This section talks about my leap into my second Year of Action at age 50.

Cape Cod, Summer 2011

My plan was to see how I felt about work when my mind was clear and relaxed at *The Brown Owl*. What did I want to do next?

We had an amazing time with incredible friends and magnificent weather. So much joy. It became clear. I knew that I would be leaving my job. Enough. I had forgotten what joy felt like. I needed to find it again. I had started to put my finances in order when it started to get bad at work. My plan was to work through the fall and be looking for another job during that time.

So much for plans.

I realized that I had to make some changes now. I needed to get joy back in my life – before it was too late.

If not, I realized that I would be on a path to becoming one of those sad people who shuffles slowly into work with their head down and no joy in their face; who just counts the days until the weekend - and until retirement. Someone who wakes up and realizes - too late - that 5, 10, 20 years have gone by and they've been at a job they don't like and have been complaining about it - every day - to anyone who will listen.

Is this what you want to subject people too – to listen to the same old complaints day in and day out? Is this the example that you want to set for your kids about what to expect in life - a series of endless *Sunday Night Blues?* You can't get these years back. Is this the kind of life you want?

I had a plan.

I started from a place of possibility. I tried to find a way to get back to doing what I had loved as well as solve some problems that the organization needed to address. I presented ideas about ways to make changes with my staff and with my role. I had a plan to help experiment without risk and a plan to connect different groups that were operating as silos and needed help, through an innovation hub, without any new staff needed.

My bosses said, "No."

They told me we couldn't do anything new, but that they did need help tagging content.

With that, I knew that the job I had was gone. It was no longer about innovation; it was about maintenance.

I smiled. I finally saw that the cage door had opened. My time here was done. It was all very calm and professional. I had loved so much of my time here, and there were so many wonderful people. It truly was about creative differences now. We were on different wavelengths with different needs now. I wasn't running away out of fear. It was just time. I talked to my husband that night and I quit the next day.

I do realize that this is *not* how you are supposed to do things. My plan had been to do what most people do and look for a job while you have one. Use your lunch hour (or free time) to search.

I couldn't do that.

One – it's not in me to do something halfway and just mail it in. I poured my heart into whatever I did and I didn't know how to be there but not really be there.

And two - I couldn't just jump into something else right away. I needed a break. I needed to take a deep breath and recharge before I could leap into something new. My battery was dead.

It was just before I made my decision that I had been fortunate to connect with Rita Foley – *from my women's group and also a Smithie!* - who, along with three others, had just written the book, *Reboot Your Life*.[13] Rita helped to counsel me and let me know I could do it.

My family was incredible. They had seen what I had been going through and I knew that they would support my decision – even if some of them secretly thought I was crazy to quit! I talked to my brother Jim quite a bit who was a fantastic coach.

Once I realized what I needed to do, the timing seemed perfect. My 50th birthday (and the 25th anniversary of my first *Year of Action*) was at the end of the month. That would be my last day of work. *Happy Birthday to me!*

Again, this approach is not normal and not my first recommendation. In a perfect world you don't quit without another job. Everyone knows that. But sometimes, life needs you to *not* follow the normal. Sometimes, it needs you to leap.

The best part of all of this though was driving home from the Emergency Room, after the pine nuts incident, on the day I quit. My son was fine and we finally had a moment of peace.

I told him I had talked to my bosses and told them my ideas for innovation and they told me that I couldn't do anything new. So I told them that I'd have to quit.

My son said, "Yeah, you have to quit."

"Why do you say that?"

"Well, Mom, your job is innovation and innovation *means* new. If you can't do anything new, that's like trying to make S'mores without any graham crackers, chocolate or marshmallows. You have to leave."

"That's exactly right honey." A simple, true moment.

2011

I had it all wrong.

My life over the past couple of years looked a lot like this:

I would start the day with no breakfast and a big cup of coffee. I would get to work about 8 a.m. At about 10 a.m. I would have some kind of muffin and more coffee. At about 1 or 2, I would realize I was hungry and grab something – usually yogurt or soup. At 6 p.m. – or later, after being seated most of the day (in meetings, in front of a computer, in my office, in my car), I would drive home and have a glass of wine. I would have a big dinner - and dessert. I would collapse on the couch with no energy and fall asleep watching TV. Only to have it start all over again in the morning.

A life of inaction - and I was exhausted.

It's easy to see how this happens and how this continues. I was tired. I was stressed. I didn't have any energy. I didn't even know where to begin to start making changes. I had so much I needed to change. It all seemed futile so I just continued doing what I was doing.

This is where the *moment* comes in.

It is at this point, when you are tired and overwhelmed and perhaps don't even believe you can change, that *moments* happen. They are screaming out at you to look and listen. Hopefully you have learned through my journey, that it is a good idea to start paying attention to these little moments and at some point something catches your attention and you stop and take a look at yourself and say, *"WHAT am I doing?"*

Then what?

For me, I finally opened the cage door and walked out smiling.

Boston, September 2011

Nourish Beginnings

Today's "Reflection for the Day" in the Boston Globe is *"Nourish Beginnings"* – Muriel Rukeyser. How apropos.

Yesterday was my last day at work. I was on autopilot. Going through my checklist. Packing up my office. Not processing that I was leaving. It was harder when I first started telling people a couple of weeks ago. Telling my staff. Holding back the tears. We've been through a lot together.

I was actually excited yesterday. I was proud that I was taking action. Taking a step. Being open to what my next chapter will be. Exploring. Recharging. Seeing my kids more.

Although, as my son was getting ready for school this morning, I said, "What do you want for lunch?" He said, "Can you wake up Dad? He makes my lunch."

And so we begin. *Ahhhh.* It feels great. Nourish it.

Boston, September 2011

One step at a time – even if you're limping

17 years ago I got married – just 3+ months after we got engaged. 111 days to be exact. And I had a concussion that left me bedridden in the middle of all the plans.

I remember being thrilled to wake up to a gorgeous wedding day, after hearing forecasts for torrential downpours all week. (Our reception was out on a boat in Boston Harbor.) I picked up my dress the night before in downtown Boston, rushed back for the rehearsal dinner, did last minute packing for our honeymoon to Greece, dropped off baskets for out-of-town guests, booked the hotel on the Internet – which was unheard of back then – and just general bride stuff. I thought *that* was a hectic time!

Last Saturday was my first Saturday home in five weeks and we had a hurricane. Over the past two weeks, I have had two trips to the Emergency Room: one for my son and the pine nuts and one for me. I fell and cut my leg open during Hurricane Irene. I turned 50. Quit my job. The kids had their first day of school. I had my last day of work.

Even after all that, I woke up yesterday feeling at peace. I had a great talk with my brother about possibilities for the future. I realized I was taking nice long breaths again. I took a leisurely stroll – more of a hobble with my stitches – with my husband and kids to the Post Office and General Store. It was a great day. I am making changes in my life.

We all lead busy lives. We cram more into our days than ever before. There is so much I haven't had time to do. Write a book. Join a gym. Create a fabulous new job that incorporates my talents and passions. Get my hair cut. The trick will be balancing the gift of time with the day-to-day responsibilities – and remembering to breathe.

Life can spin out of control. It doesn't have to. YOU can change what's not working. One step at a time – even if you're limping.

 **ACTION STEP**: Making a big change – like quitting your job – is not to be done in haste or when you are upset. Take a step away. Take a deep breath. Come up with a plan that makes sense. You don't have to have all the answers, but you do need to have a plan.

Get your finances in order. Get yourself prepared as best you can. Dream big. Be specific. Get others to help you. See your moments. Believe in the possibilities.

Surround yourself with positive people who believe in you. (This is where your relationships come into play.) Remember, those closest to you may be afraid for you and urge you to stay put. Get an impartial 3rd party to give you honest feedback as well.

Then take a step.

(And every once in while - say, every 25 years or so – you may need to *leap!*)

Live your one wild and precious life

ভ

Chapter 24

You are the *Action Hero* for your life

"The time for action is now. It's never too late to do something."
– ANTOINE DE SAINT-EXUPERY

I don't pretend to have all the answers. I also don't pretend to have a quick fix for your life. What I do have is a track record of successes when I started to see moments in my life and use them as momentum to take action. Action is the key. I truly believe that you can become the Action Hero for your life. Starting right now. You have to find the way that works best for you. Here are some things that have worked for me.

It's all in your mind

Just like my godson Henry and the *Blanket of Love*, the more you can do to get yourself into the right mindset, the more successful things will be. No one can do this but you. Moments are just there to nudge you along into that mindset – but ultimately it is up to you.

Taking action and changing your life requires work. It would be SO easy to stop taking steps when the going gets a little tough. You need the right mindset and reminders to pull you through the tough spots. You need to have something (your moments) to keep you going.

You decide.

Change your mind. Change your life.

I know that this seems too easy. All I can say is, "Prove me wrong." Try it. What have you got to lose?

What do you want to believe is possible for your life? It's all in your mind. Start believing it. Really believing it. Start taking actions that support this belief.

For example, if you say, "I'll never have enough money. I'm always broke." The theory is that this is what you are attracting into your life – via your thoughts. So change your thoughts. Try saying, "I can make the changes I need to bring money into my life."

ACTION STEP: Write down a positive belief; what you want to happen. For example, "I will find fulfilling, exciting work that provides me with the money I need." Write it down and say it out loud.

_____

_____

_____

"Our deepest fear is not that we are inadequate.
Our deepest fear is that we are powerful beyond measure."
– MARIANNE WILLIAMSON

Why *not* you?

You have more power than you realize. You can do anything. YOU are the one who decides what you can and cannot do.

ACTION STEP: Imagine your dream happening. Say it out loud. See yourself on the cover of the magazine, taking a bow on the Broadway Stage, choosing a color for your new car, looking out at the Eiffel Tower from your Paris apartment, designing the cover for your book. See it. Believe it. Why *not* you?

The science of action

In chemistry, the *activation energy* is the minimum amount of energy required to convert a normal stable molecule into a reactive molecule. Or in layman's terms, what is the *activation energy* needed to get you off the couch?

A body at rest stays at rest and a body in motion stays in motion unless some other force acts upon it. If you want to change something, you need to *change something.*

So it takes some effort, some outside force to get you going, to take action. This is the WHY; the reason that will motivate you to get up and get going when the forces of nature are compelling you to stay put. It does take some kind of energy – scientific or otherwise – but you can do it. It is so worth it. C'mon – time to get up and get going.

Inch by inch

The CFO at *That Legal Place* had a one-inch keychain that said, *"Inch by inch everything's a cinch. Taken by the yard, everything is hard."* I say this all the time. I shorten it though and just say, *"Inch by Inch."* It's a great reminder to not try and tackle everything at once. I'm not thinking that I have so much weight to lose and how hard that is, I am just thinking that I have to drink water today.

Don't think about all the things that you have to do. You just need to focus on the task at hand - which is much less daunting. Just focus on it and then the next one.

15 minutes

A lot can happen in 15 minutes. People usually think about it as your window for fame - your time in the spotlight. It can also be the amount of time you need for change to happen.

I read a story of a woman whose house was a cluttered mess. She was tired of it and told herself that she needed to do something about it but nothing changed. She kept doing the same things.

Her *moment* happened one day when she was being driven home by an acquaintance and when they walked through the front door, her friend screamed, "Oh my God, you've been robbed!"[14]

She hadn't – it was just a mess. It was a *moment*.

She took a step. She set her kitchen timer for 15 minutes and went around her house with a garbage bag and just threw things away for 15 minutes. Simple. She didn't think about everything else she had to do she just took action and got started.

It feels good to make progress: to lose a pound, to see your kitchen counters, to make a phone call, to do something towards a better day.

We have started doing this with the kids. The timer makes everyone move quickly. We make a game out of it. You can do a lot in 15 minutes.

ACTION STEP: Amaze yourself and see how much you can do in 15 minutes.

Put a pile of laundry away. Clean up the clutter in the family room. Unstack the dishwasher. Email a friend and ask her to meet you for coffee this week. Jot down some titles for your book. Do some sit-ups. Close your eyes and take a few deep breaths. You'd be surprised how much you can accomplish in a few minutes. Try it!

Write it down

You need to write things down. Not on a computer – but really write it down. You know the old fashioned way, with a pen and paper. It's easy to have a *To Do* list that has 25 (or more!) things on it. Yet, that can be discouraging if every day you look at the list and see so many things that you never get to.

Maybe it's time for a new kind of list.

I worked with someone who kept a project list with 188 things on it. 188 things! What kind of list is that? We would ask her where our project was on her list and she would say, "96."

96? Why even bother? You never get to #96. Let's be real, you never get to #20. It just serves to make everyone feel bad. You can have 188 goals but you need to break them down into smaller chunks.

I started small by taking action on things I had been putting off (hanging posters, calling the doctor). I moved on to things that I was nervous to do (taking a day off, asking for a raise). Then I started to dream big (quit my job, live in Paris). But it all started with little steps.

Writing it down makes it feel real. I broke it down into little chunks and started doing them one at a time. There is something too about the physical act of writing that helps your brain make it seem real. [15]

Once you know what you want to accomplish this year, you can break it down by what you want to happen in the next six months, three months. This month. This week. Today.

Act like it's the day before vacation

"You get an enormous amount of work done the day before vacation."
– ZIG ZIGLAR

Zig Ziglar[16] and Seth Godin[17] talk a lot about this. The day before you leave for vacation, you are laser-focused. You get so much done! You know what you need to do before you can leave. You have incentive. You cut out the fluff and the waste. You know – and do – what's important. What if you did this EVERY day?

(When was the last time you took a vacation? If you think you're too busy/important/indispensible to take a vacation – let me tell you something, "You're not!" Brain surgeons, presidents of countries, even Lady Gaga all take a break. It's not a badge of honor to say you're not taking a vacation – it's embarrassing that you can't figure it out. Don't brag about it. Don't complain about it. Figure it out! Take a long weekend. Take your kids to the beach for an afternoon. Sit on a porch and read a book. Life is short! Take a break!)

Never mistake activity for achievement

There are lots of methods and plans for being more productive. This isn't about being busier; it's about being more focused and purposeful in WHAT you are doing.

As the great Coach John Wooden said, "Never mistake activity for achievement." I have started to write down what I HAVE to do today. Focus on what is important and what has to get done TODAY.

Think about what you are doing. The goal is to find a balance between work, chores and errands while also doing things that bring positive change into your life.

Easier said than done. There is a lot of juggling in life, but there also needs to be time to *choose* what you are going to do and how you are going to live. Are you just running around like a madman? Why? If you are a parent, and spending hours driving your kids everywhere, can you figure out a better way? Share the driving with others? Limit some of the activities? Walk (and get exercise)? Have kids help with more things around the house (cooking, cleaning, setting the table, doing the dishes) to earn the right for these activities and free up some of your time? WHY are they doing all these activities? Do they need to be on 3 sports teams, playing 2 instruments and being chauffeured to meet friends? Why? It's about *consciously* deciding what makes sense for your family and how to work together to make it happen.

It's about taking a step back from your life and figuring out how to get control of your life. Who is creating your "To Do" list? (You are.) Who can change it? (You can.) One little step at a time.

 **ACTION STEP**: Ask yourself what HAS to get done today? Why is it important? If you only had 3 hours today, what would you do? What would you *not* do? Can you change the way you normally do something? Do you *need* to make 8 calls to make plans? Stop and think about what you are doing. What can you change? What one thing CAN you do today – even a small thing – that will make a difference? One call. One email. One invite. One step towards something you've dreamed of doing and then do it!

If you only had a year to live, what would you do?

You may hear people say that life is short. But have you actually stopped to think about that? You and those around you don't always have tomorrow. We are back to where we started with my first *moment*:

Life, as you know it, can change in an instant.

You can't take anything for granted.

ACTION STEP: What if you only had a year to live? What would you do? As morbid as this sounds, it actually helps you focus on what matters to you. Why aren't you doing this now? What is stopping you? What do you need? Who can help?

For me, I had lost my way over the past couple of years. I had lost my sense of joy. I had lost my confidence. I wasn't doing work that I loved. I stopped and finally asked myself: WHY?

Why am I doing this? Why am I living like this? What am I waiting for? What am I doing?

Once I took a step back and saw my life, I realized I needed to change. I started taking steps. It didn't matter what I did, as long as I was doing *something* towards change. After each step you can assess where you are and adjust as needed. But just keep taking a step and then another one.

Let's put what we've learned into action. It doesn't matter if we have different goals. You can use my goals as a guide for how to take action on your goals – the process is the same.

My *Year of Action* goals for this year are:

1) Change something. (Lose weight - 50 pounds.)
2) Create something. (Write a book.)
3) Follow my passion. (Find work that I love that also allows me flexibility and financial stability.)

Here is a summary of the key *Action Steps* throughout the book. We will be using these questions and tips to take action on our three goals.

Action Steps Summary – 20 questions:

It's easy to forget that you are in the driver's seat; easy to make excuses for NOT taking action. You can get overwhelmed and give up before you start. Here is a recap of the *Action Steps* to help you SEE your moments and BELIEVE in the possibilities for your BIG, fabulous life.

You probably know these things. There's no magic. These serve to remind you to "step back from your painting" to see things clearly and see that your life is just *waiting* for you to live it.

1. Step back. Ask yourself WHAT are you doing with your life?
2. WHY are you doing what you are doing?
3. What do you REALLY want? Are you living the life you want?
4. What are you TIRED of? What do you want to change?
5. When you LOOK BACK on your life, what do you want to have done? How is the WORLD BETTER by your being in it?
6. Write down some CRAZY, 'you've got to be kidding me', fabulous DREAMS - even if they seem impossible.
7. Look through your list. Say them out loud. PICK 3 DREAMS that you want – truly, honestly want - to happen.
8. WHY do you want these dreams? Why are they important?
9. What's STOPPING you? What are some possible solutions?
10. If MONEY were NO OBJECT, what would you do?
11. What would you do if you COULDN'T FAIL?
12. What do you LOVE/ get lost in; you stay up late to work on?
13. How do you SEE/DESCRIBE yourself? How do others see you?
14. When you had a GREAT DAY at work, what were you doing?
15. What 5 THINGS are you good at and 3 that you're not good at?
16. What would you like to do MORE OF/LESS OF at work?
17. What are the specifics of your PERFECT JOB?
18. What 5 COMPANIES do you love? Name 5 PEOPLE you admire who have fabulous jobs. Why are they fabulous?
19. What if you only had a YEAR TO LIVE? What would you do?
20. What ONE thing can you do today towards your dream?

Action Tips Summary – 25 tips to take action:

YOU decide how you want to live your life. Below are some samples of things you can do to get started, once you have your answers to the *Action Step* questions from the previous page. You CAN start to live your BIG, fabulous life by taking simple, little steps like these:

1. SAY out loud what you are going to do.
2. SEE your dream happening. Write it down. Tell someone.
3. Surround yourself with POSITIVE people. Be positive.
4. Try something NEW.
5. Give it your all. "SIGN" your work.
6. Make a PLAN. You don't need all the answers, but have a goal.
7. Ask others for HELP.
8. Do lots of FAVORS. Do something today to help someone.
9. How are you spending your TIME? What HAS to get done?
10. Say YES to one thing where you would usually say NO.
11. Say NO to one thing where you were afraid to say NO.
12. THANK as many people as you can. Be KIND. Be NICE.
13. MAKE the time. Make a call. NURTURE your relationships.
14. RECHARGE your batteries. Take a break.
15. DON'T WAIT. Imagine this is the last time you'll see someone.
16. TRY SOMETHING you think you're too old, too clumsy, too whatever to do. Get off the sidelines and JUMP IN.
17. PUSH yourself. BELIEVE in yourself. It's okay to be afraid.
18. ASK for what you want.
19. DO the work.
20. Make plans THE MOMENT you talk about doing something.
21. AMAZE yourself and see what you can do in 15 minutes.
22. STOP making excuses. Stop talking yourself out of what you need to do. GET UP and get going.
23. Don't take yourself too seriously. Go to your FUNNY PLACE.
24. YOU decide what kind of life you want to live.
25. Do ONE thing today towards your dream. You'll be amazed at what YOU can make happen.

Chapter 25

Goal # 1 –
Change something.

(Lose weight – 50 pounds.)

"To climb steep hills requires slow pace at first."
– WILLIAM SHAKESPEARE

I have set new goals for myself. I feel re-energized. I am living my life. You can too! It doesn't matter if losing weight isn't one of your goals. This example can provide a framework to help you take action on your specific goal – whether that is to clean out your garage, go to college or stop smoking. Remember that if you start thinking of everything that has to happen, it can feel overwhelming and unreachable and you may want to give up before you even start. The lizard brain is loud. But you know better than that now. You know that you don't have to listen. You can see the possibilities. You don't need to do everything at once. You just need to do one thing today towards your goal. So, where do you start?

 **ACTION STEP**: Say out loud that you want to change. Decide that you have had enough, you deserve better. Say what you DO want.

Choose a moment(s) - your WHY. WHY is this change important? WHY do you want to do this? What will you hold on to when the going gets tough?

You mean I'm *not* going to live forever?

At 50, when you get your AARP card in the mail and you suddenly need reading glasses, you realize that you are *not* going to live forever. As opposed to at age 25 when of course you are. My wake-up call at a young age with my father in the ICU, hit home hard. It was a gift though. It taught me that life is short. I didn't wait until I was 50 to realize this. I have known it all my life. Life is today. Not tomorrow. Today.

If you want to do something, you can't wait.

For the first time in my life, I also started to think about my health. I can give myself some advantages if I change my lifestyle. Not take a pill, not go on a crash diet, but change my habits. Change the way I've been doing things and start taking better care of myself. It's not that we all don't know this; we just aren't motivated to do anything about it. My hope is that you see a *moment* sooner rather than later on this one.

Middle School

Middle School was no picnic. I hated it. I was afraid to go to the bathroom because I thought I would get beat up. The "tough girls" used to hang out in there smoking. I was shy. I wore glasses. I had buckteeth. It was not fun. I haven't looked back since. Until now.

My son is in middle school. His school is fantastic and the teachers are out of this world. We came back from Parent's Night and I thought how lucky he is to be able to go to a great public school like this. But, the thing that I noticed was that I could barely fit in the desk – you know the attached chair and desk. How can that be?

Enough.

If I want to be around to see my kids, I have to do something about my health and my weight. Now.

I am 50 years old and I am going to lose 50 pounds.

I have absolutely no idea how or what to do.

I need help, professional help. I can't do this on my own but I am going to do it.

This little *moment* – sitting (squeezing) in the desk gave me one of my WHYs – my thing to hold on to when I want to quit. Some of the other whys are: I have seen others who have lost weight and I believe that I can too; I have an upcoming trip to the beach; my clothes are not fitting; the number on the scale; I am tired of living like this; and the #1 WHY - I want to be healthy and be around for my kids.

So now what? (What are your *moments* for your 1st goal?)

Now that we have our moments and believe in the possibilities, it's time to take action. Do something. Take a little step and then another. (I also like to say *Year of Action* with a fist pump too.) Instead of thinking of all the reasons why I would never lose 50 pounds, I started taking action.

- I bought some sneakers.
- I picked up a flyer for a fitness program I heard about.
- I went to the Open House – even though I didn't want to go.
- I joined the program right then at the Open House.
- I (nervously) showed up for class.
- I started working out with the class three times a week.
- I sat with a nutritionist there to help me figure out what to eat.
- I started buying better food – and stopped bringing my "trigger foods" into the house (cookies, cheese, sweets).
- I began changing what I eat.
- When I was having trouble, I told my nutritionist I was having trouble and set up an appointment to talk.
- I went to the appointment.
- I had the nutritionist specifically write out a plan that works for my lifestyle and foods that I like.
- I followed the plan – pretty closely.
- I started writing down how much water I was drinking.
- I told my friends what I was doing – which kept me accountable.
- I stumbled through the holidays and gained weight.
- I didn't punish myself or use it as an excuse to give up.

- I took a deep breath and drank a little more water and tried a little harder.
- I pushed myself to go a little farther each time on the cardio machines.
- I bought pants in a smaller size – and they fit!
- I started paying attention to what I was eating.
- I eat small portions every 3 hours and I'm not hungry for a big meal.
- I don't eat dessert – and I don't miss it. Honestly I don't. If I want a little taste, I have it and I move on – no guilt.
- I think about what I am eating.
- I realize that you need to move every day; you need to take care of your body. It's like brushing your teeth. You just need to do it. Our body is all we have.

I have been doing this for seven months – through the holidays even. I would never have believed it. I am actually going to the gym four times a week. I put my daughter on the bus and go. I don't think about it or give myself time to make an excuse. I just get up and go. I don't love going – although I do love how I feel when it's done. I physically feel so much better too. I used to be out of breath just running up the stairs – now I am running 10+ miles a week. Me? It's hard to believe – and it's all happening with little steps.

I had enough of the ups and downs - the quick losses and then the quick regaining of the weight. The slow and steady, although not glamorous, is the secret to the long-term success. Changing my life vs. taking a pill.

I don't feel like I'm on a diet or on something that has a start and finish. I am learning new habits for my life. Exercise needs to be a way of life. You only have one body. At some point you realize that you need to take care of it and the longer you wait the harder it gets.

It is also not about deprivation. I often have a glass of wine with dinner. (I did live in Paris after all.) I don't always have it but when I do, I appreciate it. If I really want dessert I have it. But I am conscious of eating it and to my surprise I often don't even want it. Or I may just want a taste and I truly enjoy that. I am not "wolfing it down" mindlessly. Plus there's no guilt after the fact or using it as an excuse to give up. It's about finding a way to work all of this into my life.

Having appointments at the gym keeps me going and accountable. People are expecting me and I just show up – that's half (or ¾) of the battle right there. It's like having a doctor's appointment – you just go. These appointments are at least as important as my daughter's basketball practice or my son's trombone lesson. Why don't we have appointments for ourselves that matter too?

I just decided that I wanted something better. I wanted to change and took a small step and then another. This goal is happening. I am on my way. I have a plan and I will continue to make adjustments as I go along. I believe it. I am doing it. Nothing earth-shattering or crazy difficult – just stringing together a lot of little steps inspired by a lot of little moments.

I believe that you can do it too. You can start making progress on your dream – today.

I hated the gym. I didn't want to think about any of it. I would just eat without thinking. I used food as a reward. I was an emotional eater. I ignored my health. I thought that this was just how it had to be.

It isn't. It doesn't have to be like this. It IS possible. You just need your moment – your WHY – and take action. One step – and then another one.

Here are some excerpts about my journey to get healthy:

September 2011

The next step

As I begin my new journey, I'm thinking about *"steps"*. Take a *step*. Watch your *step*. One *step* at a time. First *step*. *Step* by *step*. *Step* in. *Step* down. *Step* up. *Step* on it. The journey of a thousand miles begins with a single *step*.

We talk a lot about steps, yet we are a sedentary lot. We spend HOURS *sitting*. Sitting in our cars. Sitting in front of computers. Sitting in front of the TV. We are not taking enough steps – literally and figuratively. Maybe we just need to think more about *little* steps. About *next* steps.

Over the past five years, I probably went out to lunch about five times. I had lunch at work with people, but never left the grounds. Also, the majority of time I ate lunch at my desk. How crazy is that? Not even taking a real break? And for what?

So it's been funny for me that every day this week, I have been out for lunch. Sometimes coffee too. So much so that I thought, I can't do this. I want to be losing weight. I can't keep eating these big meals. Plus when people ask me to pick a place, I have *no* idea where to go. *People go out to lunch?*

Don't get me wrong. I LOVE having the time to see people. What a gift. I got home each day feeling energized. I just *don't need to eat, to meet*. So yesterday, I took a new step. I switched a lunch date to a morning walk. We met at a coffee shop. Instead of sitting, we started walking. I was out of breath trying to walk and talk at the beginning but we found a comfortable, yet brisk pace that worked for us.

(Quick aside: Knowing I wanted to get in shape, I took the first step. I bought some "workout clothes." I'm used to the old grey sweatpants, so when I put on my spandex-y shirt and saw a hole at the wrist, I was bummed that it was ripped already. Then I noticed that it was sewn that way. And there was a hole in the other sleeve too. I popped in on my nine-year-old brushing her teeth and said, "What do you think these holes are for?" Without a blink, she said, "Those are for your thumbs, Mom." How did she know that? And why do your thumbs need their own holes?)

My aunt Gail had joined a group called *Get in Shape for Women* and loved it. They had a booth at our town fall fest and I decided to go ask them about it. *Year of Action!* Another step. They didn't bite either.

They told me that they were having an Open House the following week. I took a flyer.

On the day of the Open House, I had a conflict during that time. It would have been easy to just blow it off and make an excuse that I couldn't go. *Year of Action!* I went early and asked if I could talk to someone before the Open House. They were fantastic. Hey – that wasn't bad either.

One little step at a time. I am not thinking about the long road ahead of me, I am just thinking about the next step. (I also say, "*Year of Action*" and pump my fist along with my steps so I don't chicken out or make excuses – which seems to help me.)

It's easier than you think. I dare you to try it. Before you know it, you're making changes in your life. You don't have to have all your steps mapped out either. You just need to keep taking a step and taking a breath. See where you are, make any adjustments and then do it again. Take *a step*. You don't have to get overwhelmed by thinking about ALL that you have to do to get where you want to go. Maybe you don't even know where that is. All you have to do is take a step. Any kind of step. Buy some workout clothes. *Done.* Feels good. That wasn't so hard. What's next?

 **ACTION STEP**: If you were like me and eat at your desk, don't. It's a mistake. Get up. Go for a walk. Grab a sandwich. Drag a co-worker with you. You need a break. You'll have more energy, be happier and healthier. I know you think you're showing your work ethic and your dedication, but it's pathetic. I know. Step out this week and let me know about it. I'll even give you a big thumbs up – *you know, there's a special hole for that.*

September 2011

The Before Picture

I've often heard that the hardest part of losing weight is just getting *to* the gym. I completely agree. For me, a gym is totally intimidating. I think nothing of setting up Wi-Fi, routers and networking all my gadgets, but I have no idea what any of the gym equipment is for – what I should do – how to start. So I never did.

This is why it was a big deal for me yesterday. I went to the gym and signed up for six months at *Get in Shape for Women*. One of the questions on their sheet asked me to rate how frustrated I was with my current program. I couldn't answer that. It's not as though I have tried things and they haven't worked. I haven't tried. I've ignored myself.

I love their philosophy. You make weekly appointments and you work around *those* appointments just as you would any other important appointment on your calendar - like a doctor's appointment. It's ONE hour. You show up ready to go and shower at home. I deserve ONE hour, a few times a week, for myself.

You are in small groups (1-4 people) and your group has a personal trainer for the session who takes you through it all – pushes you, helps you. They stress positive attitude and commitment before they accept you into the program. We are expected to help and encourage each other in our workout group.

My consultant actually took me through the big, scary machines. It felt great. It's one of those fears that I had never done anything about. I couldn't believe that I was actually someone who was using the machines. They have a nutrition program and I set up an appointment. I have *no* idea what I am supposed to eat.

During the sign-up session, I broke down in my consultant's office. I'm not sure why. Perhaps when I saw my body fat % number. Perhaps when I realized that things had gotten out of control and I need help. Perhaps when I realized that things actually were going to change. Perhaps, even more than quitting my job, I felt proud of myself for taking action and putting myself on my "To Do" list.

Just before leaving, we took a "before" picture. I didn't see it, but it made me believe that there will be an "after" picture. (You can see the pictures on the website: YearofAction.com.)

October 2011

Weighing In

It's been 11 days since I started going to the gym and eating better. It's amazing how quickly you can start changing your life. It's all about taking small steps. Really. Little actions can make a big difference.

I am already feeling so much better. It doesn't have to be some huge deal. I don't feel deprived. I don't feel like I'm on a diet. I am actually eating more. I don't feel overwhelmed with how much I need to lose. I just feel great.

I had my weigh-in today and I've lost 8½ pounds. I thought the scale was wrong. 8½ pounds in less than 2 weeks??!

This is not to say that it's a piece of cake – no pun intended. The workouts are tough – but doable. My muscles have been aching as they get used to actually being used! My stomach has been a bit queasy with the change in eating habits and influx of protein. The support of the other women is great. For me this program is working. I have a personal trainer (for 3-4 people at a time). I have a nutrition consultant. I have appointments that I honor as important on my calendar.

I always thought that personal trainers were for Oprah and the "Real Housewives of" wherever... But this program is the ticket for me. I'm investing in my health, my family and myself by doing this.

If I were reading this a few months ago I would be thinking, "That's great for her. She has time and money to do this. I don't. I can't." It's funny how we find excuses for *not* living the lives we want. "I can't do that." "I don't have time." "I *(fill in the blank)*." The truth is that you can – you just aren't. I'm not saying that it's easy. I'm just saying that it is possible. It would have been easy to use money as an excuse. I am not working. But I found other things I could save on. I am not going out to dinner – which is a double win! I drive an old car. I haven't been shopping in a long time. I am making choices about how I am spending my money. The expense of a gym is a lot cheaper than the hospital – which I would have landed in had I continued my old lifestyle. So I wasn't going to let money be my excuse.

For me, I hadn't been ready before. I hadn't gotten to my *moment* – my WHY. It's not about the losing weight or about reaching a certain number goal. It's about WHY are you doing this. What is the motivation? I finally have had enough. I am tired of not taking care of myself. I am tired of my clothes not fitting. I am tired of being tired. Barely fitting into the desk at the middle school? Okay, this is ridiculous – I need to do something.

What I like is that I'm not trying some quick fix that is unsustainable. It's not a magic pill. I'm not counting calories, measuring things or just eating carrot sticks. I'm just paying attention. I am changing my life. I am learning about nutrition and health. I am making it fit my lifestyle.

I'm not making excuses. If I want a glass of wine, I have one. If I want to taste the dessert, I taste it. It is about making conscious choices and being aware of what I am doing. I realize my journey is just starting – but it has started. And that is the hardest part.

 **ACTION STEP**: Have you *weighed in* on your own life lately? What changes do you want to make? What journey can you get started on today? What excuses are you telling yourself? *I can't do it because...* That's what I used to think. *Year of Action!* Get out there and get going!

October 20, 2011

50 days

Wow! 50 days. It's been 50 days since I turned 50 and quit my job. I feel like a new person.

I gave myself permission that for 50 days I would just focus on recharging. Not worry about what I was going to do next. Not start job hunting. I would take a deep breath and start working on my goal to get in shape and lose 50 lbs.

50 days seemed like a long time back then.

It reminds me of maternity leave. Before you have a baby, you have grandiose plans of what you're going to do with "all the time off." Then, when you're in the middle of it, you're lucky if you get a shower. One of my very smart friends, a seasoned mom Katie C., told me back then to just try and get *one* thing done a day – like doing a load of laundry or getting to the grocery store – and celebrate that. There is a reason why you need the time. You are not sleeping, your body is recovering and you are adjusting to life with a new baby.

I've needed these 50 days. The first month was a bit of a blur. When you're in the middle of a tough situation you don't realize the toll it takes on you. It takes about 30 days to shake yourself out of it.

I joined a health club and have lost about 10 lbs. I went from not doing ANYTHING to working out 4 times a week with a trainer. When I started, I could barely do 20 minutes on the treadmill. Now I am lifting weights for 30 minutes and running more than 2 miles at a time. In fact, I'm running more than 8 miles a week. How cool is that?

But, by far, the best has been to be here for my kids. You don't get this time back. My son turned 13 this week. I have a teenager!? From what I hear, time is really going to start flying now.

I am thrilled with my decision and haven't looked back. I'm writing a book. (Voila!) I'm designing a new education model. I'm playing the piano. I've met a Supreme Court Judge, the president of the Baseball Hall of Fame and my kids' teachers. I walk hand-in-hand with my daughter to the bus, help with book reports and French homework and get trounced, mercilessly, by my son and his Xbox.

I'm off to a conference today and to FL next week. I have had a number of people calling me about jobs and a lot of people offering to help. I am breathing. I am sleeping well. I feel happy. I don't know what my next step will be and that's okay. I'm on the right path and I'm getting there one step at a time.

October 2011

No one said it would be easy

I haven't used an alarm clock since my son was born – 13 years ago. Seems there's always someone up and my body clock has just adjusted. I wake up at 5:30 or 6 – pretty much every day.

Except today. I woke up at 7:16. My appointment at the gym is 7:30. The house was quiet – it's a Saturday. I was tired. It would have been SO easy to just stay in bed and skip the gym. This is where it matters. This is how change happens. At the times that you want to just quit and go back to bed – you have to force yourself to plow ahead.

I did. I got to the gym at about 7:35 and jumped in. I was so proud of myself for just getting there. The workout is the "easy" part. It's the "above the shoulders" part that gets in the way.

November 2011

What were you thinking?

There's a funny commercial that shows a young couple coming up with lame excuses to the question, "Did you go to the gym today?"

"Uhhhh…I forgot my ponytail holder."

"Wednesdays are weird."

"My mom called."

All your life you are told to use your head, to stop and think about what you're doing. There's one exception: *exercise*. Don't think. Just do.

Even when you make the gargantuan effort and get yourself *to* the gym, *thinking* still gets you in trouble. I can't lift those weights. I can't stay the whole hour. I can't run any faster, any longer. This hurts. This is hard. I want to stop.

You *should* stop…stop thinking.

I've been going to the gym now for 6 weeks – 3 or 4 times a week. It's 30 minutes weights and 30 minutes cardio. I know I feel great once my workout is over. I know I can do it. I know it is what I want.

Yet still, if I stopped to think about it, I wouldn't go.

On the cardio machines when I'm at about 5 minutes, I tell myself I'll never make it to 30 minutes. I can't do it.

Better to just not think at all. Just do.

The secret to cardio, I've learned, is intervals. We do 3 minutes at a good pace and then 60 seconds as fast as you can go and then back to 3 minutes at a good pace.

My machine of choice is the elliptical. It has a kind of snowshoe-type thing that you put each foot on and they go up and down and around and at the same time your arms are pulling these ski pole type things back and forth.

I was thinking about it today, during one of the fast sessions. I thought, I have NO idea how I am doing this. In fact, if I tried to think about how I was doing this, I would slip and lose my footing and go flying off this thing and bang my head and…

What?!

Better to just not think. Better to just be like Pavlov's dogs and wait for the bell. It rings when the 60 seconds start and stop. I put my head down and go. I don't think about anything.

That way, I won't let not having a ponytail holder or my mom calling get in the way of exercise. I least I don't *think* so.

ACTION STEP: We talk ourselves out of what we really want to do. Are you serious about this? Then that means doing certain things – even when you don't feel like it. No one said it would be easy. But this is precisely when you know that you're on to something - when real change is happening. When it would be so easy to throw in the towel – and you stick with it! Stop thinking. Stop making excuses. Stop talking yourself out of what you need to do. Just get up and keep going. You'll be amazed at what can happen!

November 2011

My willpower muscle is tired

I had been doing great with my exercise and eating and drinking water – then we had **two** Halloweens.

Our town postponed Halloween this year (I didn't know you could do that!) because with all the trees down and the power out with this freak snowstorm, it didn't seem safe to have kids in the streets with no lights. We were staying at my brother-in-law's house – who had power – and their town didn't cancel. So we went "Trick or Treating" on Monday.

Our Halloween was Friday night. So we went out again. I must have had 20 "little" candy bars this week. I'll just have one. Then another. Then I couldn't stop.

What happened?

Turns out my willpower muscle must have been tired.

Duke University researchers published a study this year from data that followed 1,000 young adults for 30 years and concluded that willpower is like a muscle that you can strengthen and train[18]. If you engage in high-willpower activities (exercise, learning a new language, or brushing your teeth with your other hand) you can increase levels of self-control in other areas of your life.

Willpower also requires the brain to use a lot of energy, in the form of glucose, which it doesn't have if you are hungry, tired or stressed. And just like a muscle, it can also get depleted if it's overused. You need your willpower muscle to rest and grow stronger.

So when you have a lot to do and need a lot of willpower to complete it, you may want to let it replenish by having a shorter workout that day, taking a bubble bath or having a few jelly beans – a few – not a whole bowl.

They also found that after giving in to urges (like eating 20 "little" candy bars) the best thing to do is to forgive yourself and give yourself a pep talk. It is actually worse to beat yourself up for this. You are much better off to just dust yourself off and refresh your willpower muscle.

So I'm having the kids hide the rest of their candy. I'm taking the day off from exercise. I'm ready to resume tomorrow morning at my 8:30 a.m. class.

(I'm just hoping that our town doesn't have two Thanksgivings!)

November 2011

Loving the tortoise

You know the story: The hare and the tortoise race. The hare dashes out to a mighty lead and, quite certain of his win, takes a nap in the sun. Meanwhile the tortoise, plodding along at a slow and steady pace beats the snoozing, boastful bunny.

Yes, the tortoise wins and all – but *slow and steady*? Where's the joy in that? Who wants to be the tortoise?

I got back from the gym this morning and after 9 ½ weeks I have lost 9 ½ pounds. The tortoise in me says, "That's great." Yet, the hare in me wants more. Especially since for the last 4 weeks or so I have only lost about a pound!

I can feel that I am getting in shape. I know my clothes seem bigger. I am not out of breath running up stairs. I'm "running" – or "elliptical-ing" – 2.8 miles a session. I could barely make 1.5 miles when I started.

Being the geeky data gal that I am, I made a little chart that shows that if I keep "tortoise-ing" along – at a pound a week – I will have lost 50 pounds by my birthday. Which would be great. Hard to believe - but great. So why am I complaining?

It seems like most of us embrace the hare – and begrudgingly acknowledge the tortoise in us. We'd rather take a pill and be done, rather than change our habits. Who wants to embrace something "for the long haul?"

It can be so daunting at times. But Aesop was trying to tell us something. Being a hare all the time doesn't work. It fizzles out. No wonder there are so many yo-yo dieters, or people who quit smoking for a few weeks at a time. We need to find a way to get joy from slow and steady, from celebrating a pound at a time. In this fast-paced, 'harebrained' world – we need to start loving the tortoise.

December 2011

My first road race

I am putting my new healthy workouts to a test today. I am running my first race, *The Angel Run*. Well, that's not entirely accurate. Many, many, many years ago I did a couple 2-mile fun runs (although it is hard for me to put "fun" and "run" together in the same sentence). And once, when my sister and I were dating runners (and then married them!) we stumbled through a 7-mile run – and swore that we would never do that again.

But this is my first attempt in a very long time. It is a 3.2-mile race. I can do this on a treadmill but I have not tried it in the great outdoors. I am a little nervous actually.

For the runners out there, I know this seems like nothing. You can roll out of bed and run twice as far. But for me, this is a big deal. I had pretty much crossed running off my list. I can't do it. I was out of breath running (fast walking) to the bus stop at the end of the street.

If nothing else, it feels great to knock a "can't" out of my life. I am changing. Break a leg – well…wish me luck! *Year of Action!*

December 2011

Middle of the Road

Well, I am officially a "runner" - or a "finisher" anyway. I finished my first 5K Road Race on Sunday – which seemed highly unlikely to me during my first mile. It was a lot tougher than being inside on a machine.

It wasn't pretty, but I did it!

I just checked the posted results. Of the 1200 runners, I finished in the middle (712). The funny thing is that in my division (Women 50+), I came in 32.

Getting bumped into the 50+ bracket (vs. 40 – 49) really helps. Putting it in context though, there were only 71 in my division. So again, right in the middle.

People don't aspire to be in the middle – but it's a start.

It wasn't easy. I am not naturally a runner. But I am trying. I am taking action. I am off the couch and away from my computer. It's all about taking little steps – one at a time – even if they put you in the middle of the road. My goal was to finish – and not to finish last!

(It gives a whole new meaning to "Loving the Tortoise.")

January 2012

Lucky 13

I recently booked a flight for a retreat later this winter. The only seats available were premium seats up front or way in the back in rows 30 and higher. Then I saw that there was a seat open in row 13.

I don't like to fly. I don't let it stop me but I don't like it. I did stop and consider how I would feel being in unlucky 13 but my fiscally aware (i.e., unemployed) self chose it – rather than pay a premium for an already expensive seat. Since it was available, I assume other travellers may be superstitious too. (Much like there being no floor 13 in a hotel.)

I didn't give *13* any more thought until this morning.

Typically we weigh in at the gym once a week. For the past 5 or 6 weeks I have not lost a pound. I know people talk about plateaus, about patience, about muscle weighing more than fat, about it not being about a number. But c'mon, I am at the gym 3 or 4 days a week. I am eating well. I am drinking water. That is a LONG time to go with not losing anything.

I weighed in on Thursday. Nothing.

Usually there's a lot of reminding (nagging) to get women on the scale weekly. So they may have been surprised when I asked to get weighed again this morning after having just gotten weighed two days ago. I just had a feeling…

13 pounds! I finally broke my 6-week stall out at 9-10 pounds. Then I also realized that this is my 13th week at the gym. So I can forget all those crazy superstitions, 13 feels great. I just hope I don't see any black cats today – knock wood.

February 2012

I know, I know

There are certain things everybody knows. For example, everybody knows you're supposed to: *Get a good night's sleep. Drink plenty of water. Eat right. Exercise.*

But we don't.

Start the excuses. I know them well: *I'm too busy. I don't like water. I don't have time to exercise. I eat right, well sort of. I get 6 hours of sleep and 2 glasses of water – that's close enough. I'm fine.*

Even now with the changes I have been making in my life I thought I was doing fine. I have been exercising and eating right and wondering why I had stalled out losing weight. I thought I was drinking plenty of water and getting enough sleep. How much can that really matter anyway?

Turns out a lot.

Seems that the magic number is 8. You are supposed to get at least 8 hours of sleep a night and drink 8 glasses of water. I figured I was pretty close to that.

I started to track how many glasses of water I was drinking a day. If you had asked me I would have said 8. In reality, it was more like 3. Yes 3 is better than 0 but after all the hard work I was doing to get to the gym and to eat right, it seems crazy to slack off on the "easy" stuff – water and sleep.

ACTION STEP: It takes work to remember to drink water but the rewards are amazing. I usually hear, "I know, I know but..." Water is one of those things that is so great for you. Everything works better if you have water. Plus it fills you up so you aren't eating as much. Even though *you know it,* I urge you to do it. Drink up.

April 2012

A new normal

I am changing the way I live. It doesn't have a start and stop. I am not "on" a diet. I am changing old habits. One day at a time. I am not thinking about the long haul. I am thinking about what I need to do today. I get up and exercise first thing in the morning before I have time to think about it. I get it "out of the way."

Losing weight is a goal for many people. Yet we do things to sabotage ourselves. We want the pill. We want to eat whatever we want, not exercise and magically be in shape. It doesn't happen that way. Plus, it gets even harder as you get older. Giving up or ignoring it doesn't make it go away either.

But with some little steps, you can make some big changes. It is happening. I believe in the possibilities. I am taking action. I have lost 20 pounds, 4 inches off my waist and 2.5 inches off my arms. I have lowered my body mass index/body fat. I am getting healthy. I am doing what I never thought I could do. I am certainly not perfect. But I have my WHYs, my moments that help pull me through and regain momentum when I veer off the path. I feel funny now when I don't go to the gym. I would never have thought I would say that.

I started coaching my daughter's softball team. (I wouldn't have been able to even run the bases last year.) I am losing weight and keeping it off. I am taking steps and making progress towards my goal. You can too!

It's my *new* normal – one step at a time.

May 2012

The big, white bag

I have been going along and doing well and incorporating exercise into my life. I just do it and I even feel funny now when I don't exercise. But the eating thing is tougher. It is SO easy to slip back into old habits. I am fine when I am home and can prepare food – and not buy my "trigger" foods. But this has been party season with family celebrations and graduations and birthdays. I find myself just falling back to my old ways.

I have lost 25 pounds. Which is great. But I'm stuck. I need a new incentive, something to keep me going. I am not in "maintenance" mode yet. It is easy to think, "I've lost 25 pounds – that's pretty good. I can ease up." Yet I still need to be losing weight. I need to rejuvenate my moments to keep me going.

I had an idea.

In the way back of my closet is a big, white bag. I haven't opened it in 17 years. It's my wedding dress.

The other day I took a deep breath, opened the bag and tried on the dress. It didn't fit. Not even close. You mean, I have lost 25 pounds and my dress *still* doesn't fit? I have my new moment.

I want to fit back in my wedding dress.

I had my daughter take some pictures of me in the dress. Instead of my goal being just about a number, I want to have it mean something. Does it really feel any different whether it's 40 pounds or 50 pounds? Or 32 for that matter? What is going to keep me going? I need my WHY. I want to fit back in the dress. (You can see the pictures on the website: YearofAction.com.)

June 2012

It's not a diet

I met with my nutritionist at the gym again. I had to write down what I was eating for a week. (It took me about three weeks to do this.) We made some tweaks into what I was doing. Again, it's not a diet that I am "on" that I will be "off" soon – or stopping. The whole point of picking a big number (like 50) or "fitting into my dress" is I am working on transforming my life, not just a quick pill and then back to my old ways. I need to make some life changes – and figure out a way to have them be part of my "new" way of living. A *Year of Action* way of living.

July 2012

Take a day off.

Part of my nutrition program is to take a "day off" each week. You're not supposed to go crazy, but it helps you get through the week knowing that if you *really* want to have that cookie, or glass of wine, or chocolate (anything), you can. It's just in moderation. You can have it on Saturday – or Wednesday. You decide each week.

I wasn't taking a day off. Mostly, I thought that I might fall back into my old ways and not be able to stop. Also, if I didn't take *one* day off – then I could have a glass of wine here and some ice cream there. This was a mistake. You end up eating *more* this way and undo the good work that you are doing.

So it's summer. Our schedules are all over the place anyway. I'll give it a try. I'll take a day off. I'll change it up.

I had been struggling for months (months!) at 20-23 pounds. That gets discouraging working out every week and eating well but STILL not losing weight. I wasn't eating enough. I wasn't taking a day off. I wasn't doing the little things.

I had started to tell myself that I couldn't do it. I stopped believing. I took a deep breath and started to believe again. I let go of my doubts. I took a day off. I ate more. I broke my plateau. I lost 7 more pounds.

I thought someone was messing with the scale. I kept losing weight. Who's touching the scale? This is NOT funny guys.

But it was right. When I let go and believed, I started losing again.

August 2012

I'm not going to make it.

I did the math. I am not going to lose 50 pounds by the end of August. (Actually I had started *doing the math* in the spring when I was stuck at about 20 pounds and it started to seem unrealistic that I would magically make it to 50 pounds by my birthday, but I kept going.)

I would get discouraged after hearing women talk about losing 68 pounds in 3 weeks eating chocolate or being on the "miracle of the week diet" and dropping 6 dress sizes in an hour and a half. Well, perhaps those weren't their exact results, but it sounded like that to me.

I made a choice that I didn't want to do a short-term, quick loss method. My experience had been that as soon as you stop, all the weight comes back – and more. I had to find something that could fit my life. Something that was easy for me. Not lots of crazy preparation or counting or feeling deprived. It had to be a simple way of life, which I have found with this program. Funny thing though, TRANSFORMING your life takes time. And you need to find ways to get you through the snags and over the hurdles.

The last few months were discouraging. I was working out, eating right and stuck. I haven't reached my goal. What am I doing wrong?

Well, missy, take a step back for a minute. 50 pounds is a big deal.

Do you know how much that is? I lost sight of all the great work that I *have* done. I am in shape! I coached softball. I am not out of breath. I have lost nearly 5 inches off my waist. I have muscles. But still, it's not the "number" I want.

August 30, 2012

A gallon of milk

Do you know how much a gallon of milk weighs? It weighs eight pounds. I know this because my husband filled up empty milk jugs with water and tied them together and said, "Pick this up."

It was heavy. There were 4 of them. He said, "*That's* how much weight you have lost! You had been carrying all that around 24 hours a day – all that has been extra stress on your knees, ankles, heart."

Try it. It's pretty powerful. I keep these milk jugs in my office as a great reminder.

Then I got this email on my birthday from the new manager of the gym:

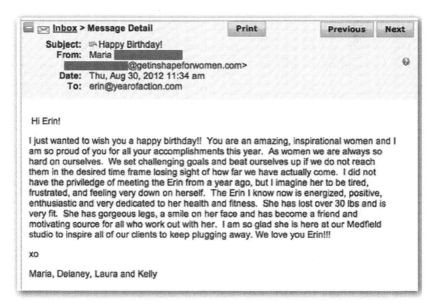

Wow. Number *schmumber*. I've changed my life. I'm on my way.

We all want the magic pill; to think that there's a shortcut to all of this. But guess what? There's no shortcut and it's *not* about a number. Don't get me wrong, I still have my goal and I still want to reach it. But it's more than that. It's about creating a new way of life.

It's overwhelming if you take it all at once. I'm not thinking, "I have to exercise for the REST of my life?" I'm thinking, "Okay, I'm going to go to my workout today." Or, "I'm going to play basketball with my kids, or walk to the library."

It's about taking it one day at a time. It's about being conscious of what you're eating. Enjoying it. Making small changes. Getting up and just moving - whether it's taking the stairs, going for a walk around the block after dinner or standing up and stretching every two hours at your computer. It's about taking an active part in your health. It can't be taken for granted. It's all we have. You need to find things that work for you. You just have to start.

I used to tell myself excuses. *I can't do it. I don't have time.* Now I make time. I choose to make it a priority. I get this "out of the way" in the morning. Everything is better when I start my day with exercise. (Believe me I *never* thought I would say that. "Never say never.") I am making a conscious choice. I am choosing to live a BIG, fabulous life. I feel less stressed. I have more energy. I feel much better about myself.

My membership to the gym is up for renewal. It is expensive. I have not worked (let me rephrase), I have not brought in money for a year. I toyed with quitting the gym. I'm on my way. I could do this on my own.

I know myself. I need the accountability. I need the appointment. I am not ready yet. I need to figure out a way to pay for it. I spoke with the gym and worked out a payment plan that works. My health is a priority. It is only going to get harder as we get older. No excuses. I renewed my membership. Keep going. One step at a time.

⚘

The next section is my journey towards my second goal, *Create something*. (Write a book.) Even if this isn't one of your goals, it can help you as a framework for how to turn ideas into action.

Chapter 26

Goal # 2 –
Create something.

(Write a book.)

"If you hear a voice within you say 'you cannot paint',
then by all means paint and that voice will be silenced."
– VINCENT VAN GOGH

I always dreamed that I would write a book. Although, like with other things in my life, it wasn't something that I ever thought that I could do. But I loved to write and just kept writing.

I started by taking a small step. The morning after my cancer surgery, I woke up early and decided that enough talk – time to act. I started a blog. I wrote one paragraph and I hit *Publish.* I was on my way to becoming a writer! It just took a *moment.*

I started to get positive feedback on my blog. People were telling me that I could write. I wrote more. I went online and found a template for writing a book. I typed out the title and the byline. When I saw my name on the page, it seemed real – yes I can write a book. I was in the library and I looked around. I was surrounded by *thousands* of books, all written by people who had to start somewhere too.

I just started writing. I found my journals from 25 years ago. I started taking excerpts from them. I was inspired by some of the things that I had done. Did I really live in Paris? Did I actually do these things that I had only dreamed about? Was that really me? Where had she gone? If I had followed my dreams once, I could do it again.

Turning ideas into action

There are so many people who have great ideas and big dreams. So, why do so many dreams and goals never happen? How do you go from thinking about something to actually making it happen? From dreaming of writing a book, to actually having it published.

The lizard brain will tell you that you can't do it; that you're not good enough, smart enough, talented enough, *whatever* enough. *"What makes you think you could do that job anyway?"*

Hopefully now though, you know not to listen.

 **ACTION STEP:** You *can* do it. It is possible. There is no magic. Turning ideas into action is not *easy* – but it is *simple*. It starts with you finding your moments, your "why". Why is this dream, this idea, important to you? Why do you want it? What are your *aha* moments – both big and small - that are tugging at you, perhaps, screaming at you, to see them? What will you hold on to when the journey gets tough?

Some of my moments that I am holding on to are:

1. Dream big and be specific. (You *can* write a book.)

2. Just be yourself. (Write what you know.)

3. Find what you love – you can figure out later how to make it work. (Don't fight it – just keep doing what you love.)

4. You do belong here but you have to actually *do* the work. (Put the time in. Write. Write. Write. Do the hard work.)

5. Find and nurture deep relationships.
(Tell somebody. Have them keep you accountable. Ask for help. Show them your work, your ideas. Ask for feedback. Listen. Act.)

6. Choose joy. (Do what makes you happy.)

I am not writing a book to make money. I am writing it because I have to write. I love it. I have always dreamed of writing a book. The time is now. I need to get it out.

I want to help to inspire others. I want to show that if I can do it, you can do it. I want others to start living their BIG lives. I want to put my money where my mouth is. Practice what I preach. Show that I am on the tough journey too. I am finding my way – finding the next chapter of my life.

The next step is to believe in the possibilities. Say it out loud. See it happening. Picture yourself doing it; completing it. Imagine the title. Imagine the cover of the book. Imagine the book signing.

 **ACTION STEP**: Once you have your moments and believe in the possibilities, it's time to act. Take a step. Do something. Tell someone. Do a little test. Write a paragraph. Create a pilot of your idea. Ask somebody what they think. Make changes. Take a step. Then another one. You're on your way.

Here is how I started believing in the possibilities and taking little steps to *create something – my book!*

- I was writing a blog, which I have loved but I wasn't writing as much as I wanted to. I started writing more frequently.
- I started getting positive feedback. People told me I should write a book.
- I started to let myself dream about that possibility.
- I dug out my old journals from my trip 25 years ago.
- I started writing, with no real formatting, just writing.
- I started to believe that I could do this.
- I told people I was writing a book.
- I came up with titles – and subtitles.
- I showed some close friends & family the initial draft.
- I asked for direct, honest feedback.
- I listened.
- I completely reorganized the entire book from their feedback and it is SO much better.

- I started getting up every day at 5 a.m. before the kids got up, to start writing.
- I wrote 300 pages in three months.
- I decided to add *Action Steps*.
- I started researching publishing options.
- I created an account on Amazon's service, CreateSpace.
- I chose and downloaded a standard size, publishing template.
- I designed some draft cover designs.
- I printed a draft cover out and "wrapped" it around a "real book" on my desk– for inspiration that this would one day be a book too.
- I found out about and bought a block of ISBN numbers online.
- I read articles from those who had written books and learned from their experiences.
- I continually saved my book on my hard drive, on flash drives and "in the cloud" so I wouldn't have to worry about "losing" the book if anything happened to my computer.
- I got consumed by writing. I got "in the zone". The words just started pouring out of me.
- I got a little too much in the zone. All I wanted to do was sit and write. I wasn't calling family or friends.
- My brother had to talk me out of the zone.
- I started tapping into my resources. I asked some close friends to help me with edits.
- I cut pages and pages out – with more cuts likely to come.
- I emailed authors I know and asked for their feedback.
- I am doing what I love. I am having a ball.
- I designed some more cover ideas.
- I posted the covers online and asked for feedback.
- I chose a cover design.
- I wrote the copy for the cover.
- I wrote the Dedication.
- I wrote the Acknowledgements.
- I wrote About the Author.

- I talked to a friend who convinced me to put the book down and wait until I finished the year – to see how my year ends!
- I put the book down for a couple of months. (This was when I realized that I had found something I love.)
- I researched ways to market the book.
- I am going to self-publish the book - for a variety of reasons.
- I will publish the book in the fall.

I look forward to signing your copy of this book so we both have proof that it can happen; dreams can come true – for me and for you!

I do also have to make money. Which brings me to Goal #3.

Chapter 27

Goal # 3 – Follow your passion.

(Find work you love.)

"Having a happy working life is not reserved for women with connections, education, chemical makeup or money; it is reserved for women who act."

– JOANNE GORDON

I want to find work I love, that is flexible and gives my family financial stability. I want to put my talents to good use. I want to work with people who love what they do, who want to do good work, who check their egos at the door and want each other to succeed. I want to work on something that makes a difference. I want to be happy.

This is not an Urban Myth. Work like this exists. I have seen it. I have been part of it – and I know *it* is out there. I want to find it again. Or start my own "it." But all this takes work. It takes action.

As with the other two goals, this one could also seem impossible at the beginning. It takes work to find what you love.

It is easy to settle, especially when you need money. I know. I've been there. It would be easy to listen to my lizard brain that is saying, "There are no jobs in this economy. Take the first one that comes along and be thankful. There are good, smart people out of work, what makes you think you are different? How will you ever find a job?"

This trap would be easy to fall into – yet some of my *moments* help to remind me that I don't have to settle. I do, however, have to do the work, the hard work, to get what I want.

Some of the moments around this goal are:

1. Find what you love. You can figure out later how to make it work.

   ACTION STEP: Start paying attention to what makes you feel happy; feel alive. Write down the things that you have loved in other jobs; what do you love now? Pay attention to what you don't love; what drains you; what makes you gain/lose energy and joy.

2. Some things are just a means to an end – do what you need to do.

   ACTION STEP: You can start making money without having to commit to full-time work. Find some consulting or part-time work, ideally in an area that you've always wanted to try. Taking a job – even if it is giving out peanut butter in a supermarket – gives you some breathing room. Sometimes you may have to take a lower-paying job to get to the job that you ultimately want – but know that it is just a means to an end.

3. You do belong here – but you have to actually *do* the work.

   ACTION STEP: Make some calls. Meet for coffee. Take the time to write down what a dream job looks like. Put the work in to get the work of your dreams. It doesn't just magically happen – but it does happen, if you put in the effort.

4. Dream big and be specific.

ACTION STEP: Write down specifics of what you are looking for. Go crazy. Go big. Dream. If you couldn't fail, what would you do? When do you feel most alive? If money were no object, what would you do?

5. Never say never.

ACTION STEP: Try new things. Don't make quick judgments. Be not afraid. You never know where something will lead. Be open to possibilities.

6. Find and nurture deep relationships.

ACTION STEP: Tap into your relationships. Ask for help. Ask for advice. Ask to be introduced. Offer to help others. Tell others what you are doing. Ask for feedback. Listen. Act.

So where do you start?

Be Happy at Work

Joanne Gordon wrote a wonderful book, *Be Happy at Work – 100 Women Who Love Their Jobs and Why*[19]. She interviewed women from all walks of life - across all kinds of industries – who LOVE their jobs. (I had never even heard of many of the jobs – like picking the music for movies or being a hospital clown.)

Their jobs were dramatically different but what she found was that all of the women who loved their jobs, loved them for three main reasons: *Process, Purpose and People* – not necessarily in equal amounts but they all had some levels of all three.

- **Process:** They find joy and excel at the *tasks* of their job. They get lost in the work; the activity itself is the reward.
- **Purpose:** They feel good about *why* they do the tasks, a purpose or mission they believe in; it is emotionally rewarding.
- **People:** They like (or at least respect) their bosses, coworkers and customers.

I often hear people say that they would follow their passion, if they only knew what it was. Again, it comes back to action. You need to do the work to find the work. There are ways to discover what you love – but you don't discover it by sitting around. You need to act. You need to try things and test things out.

Specifically, what Gordon says is that in addition to the three P's (Process, Purpose and People), the women were also all **Proactive** – they took **ACTION** – took control of their lives and career.

Gordon divided these actions into seven steps:

1. Know what you want
2. Ask for what you want
3. Reinvent the rules
4. Seek support
5. Explore – don't ignore – instinct and coincidence
6. Weigh the sacrifices
7. Exude confidence

This is a great list and like anything else, you just need to start – take a step. I always have a notebook (or two) around. I started writing down what I wanted. I started thinking about what I got lost in – things that I loved doing, where the hours flew by. I started writing down what I was good at; my marketable skills. I started dreaming – big. What would be a crazy, fabulous job? WHY is it crazy fabulous? If money were no object, what would I do? If I couldn't fail, what would I do?

My next step is to start talking to people. Start telling them about the types of things I think I would like to do and get their input. Since I need to make money, my plan will include taking on some kind of short-term work – ideally in an environment I am interested in. This is a great opportunity to test out things. You don't know if you like something until you try. If I hadn't started temping at Spinnaker Software, I wouldn't have known that I had an aptitude for technology.

One thing they don't teach in schools is the value of relationships; who you know. This is one of your most precious assets. You need to nurture your relationships. You can't just neglect them until you need something either. You need to be caring and feeding your relationships when you don't need or want anything. Do lots of favors. Help people whenever you can. Want nothing in return.

The world is becoming a smaller place. Technology allows people to connect to others in ways that would have been impossible before. There is a smart way and a not so smart way to do this though.

 **ACTION STEP**: When asking for favors or looking for work, don't forget your manners. Don't become a taker. It's a two-way street. How can YOU help them? It's not just about what *you* want – what can you do for them? How can you help the company meet its goals? Imagine you already worked there, what could you do today to start contributing? Instead of *telling* them, can you *show* them? What if you took action and did a mockup of a new homepage, updated their messaging, put together a video? SHOW them how amazing you are.

If you want to be the *Action Hero* for your life – you need to act. Taking action takes work. It would be MUCH easier to sink back into a world of excuses and complain about life and not take responsibility – to blame someone else for your circumstances. "I don't have..." "I can't." "I'm stuck." "I don't have a choice."

You have the power to open the cage door. You have the power to get out and to start living your life. I am not just preaching this – I am living it. I put my money where my mouth is. I took a big leap this year. I quit my job. I want something more. I want something better. I want to find the joy that has been missing lately. I am finding it – little by little. You can too. I am not saying that you have to take drastic measures. You just have to take a step.

I'm an idiot

When you're out of work, it is easy to lose your confidence. You can start to feel like you don't know what you are doing and you can start the downward spiral of "Woe is me." "Who would hire me anyway?" "I have lost all my skills." "I'm an idiot."

I can see how that happens – but nip that in the bud now.

ACTION STEP: You do have things to offer. Astound people. You are an *Action Hero* for your life – if you choose to be. Remember though, you have to act. You have to *do* something. Today. You need to take a step. Send an email. Pick up the phone. Do something nice for someone. Get up and go for a walk. Do not sit and surf the Internet all day long. Stay active.

This time is precious. It may be tough and discouraging at times but you will get through this. It's easy to be afraid. That's okay too. It *is* scary. But you can do it. Remember, you have to *do* the work to *get* the work. Get up and get going. Do the *Action Steps*. Ask yourself some key questions: What do you really want? What's stopping you? What are some possible solutions?

ACTION STEP: Get talking to your network - in person if you can. If you don't have a network, start building one. Connect with one person. One step at a time. So many of the great jobs will come from the people you know. The jobs may never even get posted. Don't just sit there at your computer. Take a friend to coffee. You need to put the word out there about you.

ACTION STEP: Dream big and be specific. Make it easy for people to understand what you are looking for – so that when they hear of something, they will think of you. Volunteer in the field you are interested in. Take a part time job to bring in money – do the hard work to get to the work that you love. *Year of Action!* I am right there with you. I believe in you.

Boston, April 2012

Now what?

I haven't figured out what I am going to do next. I have taken a couple of freelance jobs to start bringing in money. I have been working on a new education model. For some reason, I haven't been able to really take a step on this. Something is holding me back – but I'm not sure why. I entered the idea into an entrepreneurial challenge contest. (Dream big and be specific.)

The early returns look like it will NOT be one of the winners. Which is a good thing. Entering the contest forced me to get specific about my idea. It made me realize that my current concept is NOT what I would love doing. It helped me to make adjustments and changes to my original idea. Act. Assess. Adjust.

Boston, May 2012

I didn't win – luckily

I got my rejection letter. My entry into an entrepreneurial challenge did not win – and I feel relieved. Quite happy, actually. I was trying to fit something in a box that seemed to make sense on the surface but after taking action – and entering the contest – I realized that it was not "my" dream. It was an easy next step – but my heart wasn't in it. It's easy to want to just grab on to something, even if it's not right.

We are creatures of habit. Not having the habit of "going" to work takes some getting used to. It's easy to get lost without a typical 9-5 structure; easy to get overwhelmed with all the choices. At first you are like a kid in a candy store – running from one thing to the next - exhilarated that you actually don't have to "go" into work everyday. Then you need to catch your breath, come up with a plan and start taking steps. I get up and "work" every day, I am just not getting paid.

I feel truly blessed to have this gift of time. There is also a lot of pressure not to waste it. But I don't want to hop into the old me; to fall into my old habits, into my old work life. I took my own advice and did the *Action Steps* about finding work that you love.

Boston, May 2012

Right in front of me

I watched a video of a woman making money doing what she loved; doing a lot of what I like to do. It suddenly dawned on me that I have loved writing so much and love this *Year of Action* topic that maybe there is something here. Maybe there's a way to make THIS my work.

It has been staring me in the face for 8 months and I am only now beginning to "see the moment." It was only when I put the book down and took a step away from it that I started to see it clearly. (Have you stepped back from your painting lately?)

THIS is what I love. THIS is what I want to do. And just like not knowing how to lose weight, or how to write a book, I have no idea how to make this my work. I don't know what to do or where to start.

But that doesn't stop us *Action Heroes* does it? I've seen the moment. I need to start believing in the possibilities and take a step.

Boston, June 2012

Take a step

I absolutely love working on anything connected to the book. I need to figure out how to turn this passion into a way to also bring in money.

Maybe I could take portions of the idea that I entered into the entrepreneurial challenge contest that I (and the judges) really liked and reshape those into work that I love.

I need help. I am thinking about taking a class to help me get all these pieces to make sense; yet the money scares me. I don't want to let "money" be an excuse for not doing it. I can break the payments into smaller chunks and I can figure out a way to absorb that. It feels like a good investment. I need help from those who have done it before me.

Instead of thinking and wondering and doubting whether I can do it, I am going to start taking steps and getting some help. It is a little scary though not to have a steady stream of money coming in.

Boston, July 2012

Start before you're ready

Fear has a powerful grip. When you're afraid and don't know how to start and don't have all the answers, it is easy to sit and get stuck.

I was all over the place. I didn't know how to take a step. I needed help – so I took a class and came up with a plan. I want to start some kind of company around *Year of Action*. I'm still trying to figure out exactly what I am going to do. I keep taking little steps.

I still get job listings and part of me wishes that I would just find a "regular" job. Yet every time I see a listing, my stomach turns a little. I'm afraid of jumping back into old habits; of being chained to a desk without flexibility and not being in charge of my own life. So, as tough as it is to pursue something else, I know I want to live a BIG life. I don't want to settle. I will do the hard work to make it happen.

I called a friend and told her that I had an idea I wanted to discuss– even though I didn't have all the details ironed out. Taking action, even when you're not quite ready, forces you to make decisions and start to get clear. Putting it out there and saying it out loud, really helps. Each time you do, you get a little clearer. You get feedback. You make progress. Act. Assess. Adjust.

Boston, September 2012

Connect the dots - *Year of Action U*

"You have to believe that the dots in your life will somehow connect in your future. Believing this will give you confidence to follow your heart even when it leads you off the 'well-worn path' and that will make all the difference."
                    - STEVE JOBS

It is official. My *Year of Action* has come to a close – but it's not over. I want to bring it to life. I want to connect the dots in my life (technology, business, education, creativity, helping women) to create a new kind of *Girlfriend MBA* that teaches you how to use the new tools in business and technology, to take action and get results in life.

At a time when many people are discouraged, having spent so much time, money and effort to get an education, only to graduate without the skills they need to find a job - let alone a job they love - it is imperative to find new ways to help people take action on their lives.

I know how to turn ideas into action. I love inspiring and helping women – especially with business issues and ideas. I have an amazing network of accomplished women and I would love to bring their collective wisdom to the world, as online classes and resources. I want to help you continue to take action, long after you've finished this book. So, I took a step in that direction, to connect all of these dots, and I started *Year of Action U*.

Year of Action U is a new kind of *Girlfriend MBA* that has simple, down-to-earth explanations that are like talking with your girlfriends. It makes it easy to understand - and put into action - the new business and technology tools needed for success in today's jobs.

It can help you round out your education with practical tools, tips, real-life stories and advice on how to take action and get results in business and in life. It's learning by connecting with others and by taking action.

The secret to all that we've talked about is *continued* action – to keep taking steps even when it seems impossible and you want to give up. *Year of Action U* is a way to keep the momentum going and to help you when you get stuck. It is a community to support and motivate you; to inspire and advise you; and to help you take action to make a difference, make a living and create your BIG, fabulous life.

My *moment* for this happened after having coffee with some girlfriends who were asking me about ways to help them with things they were stuck on in their business. I realized that it didn't matter where I was - at a bridal shower, cocktail party, standing in line, or having coffee - when I told someone I quit my job and was writing this book, their eyes would light up and they would say, "I *need* that book!"

I would ask them why. Many people had "seen their moments," and knew what they wanted to do to live their BIG, fabulous life, but they didn't believe in the possibilities and didn't know where to begin. They were stuck – usually around business and technology issues.

They would ask me about writing a book, starting a blog, starting a business, using social media, getting new customers, creating videos, turning an idea into action, using new technologies and more. I would give them simple explanations and action steps to get started and their faces would light up, when they started to believe in the possibilities and had the beginnings of their action plan. I loved it. I was so energized by these connections.

It hit me. *This* is what I need to do on a bigger scale. So I took a step and started *Year of Action U.* It's part business school, part self-improvement, part Girls Weekend.

It is a work in progress. I don't pretend to have all the answers. But, I do know that amazing things happen when you start seeing, believing and taking little steps. Keep experimenting. Keep taking steps. Keep taking action.

ଓ

Losing weight. Writing a book. Living in Paris. Starting companies. I had NO idea how I was going to do these things. They all seemed completely impossible and out of reach. But hopefully you've seen that you just start by following the *Year of Action* process: See the moment. Believe in the possibilities. Take a step...and incredible things will start to happen. I'm living proof. You can be too.

It's been an amazing year and the journey is really just beginning. I want to bring this *Year of Action* way of life into your life. Please come check out *Year of Action U* at **YearofAction.com** and let me know what you think.

Chapter 28

If you had your life to live over…

"Many people die with their music still in them. Why is this so?
Too often it is because they are always getting ready to live.
Before they know it, time runs out."

- OLIVER WENDELL HOLMES

There is a palliative care nurse who spent several years caring for patients in the last 12 weeks of their lives. She recorded their dying epiphanies in a book called *The Top Five Regrets of the Dying*.[20] She asked her patients if they had any regrets or anything they would do differently and there were five themes that surfaced again and again:

1. I wish I had the courage to live a life true to myself and not the life others expected of me; that I had followed my dreams.
2. I wish I hadn't worked so hard and missed out on so much of life.
3. I wish I had the courage to express my feelings.
4. I wish I had stayed in touch with my friends.
5. I wish I had let myself be happier.

Live your life - today

These five regrets can serve as powerful moments for all of us. Life is so precious and yet it is so easy to forget that. We put off our life. We get lazy. We get into routines; into bad habits; into ruts. We stop seeing our *moments*. We stop believing in the possibilities. We stop taking steps. We live a life of inaction.

But you have the power to change all that. Right now. Today.

You have seen my journey to a *Year of Action* way of life. It is a journey of 25 years, 9 countries, 9 jobs, 1 marriage, 2 kids... and it is still going. You have seen big and little moments that I used as the momentum to take action and to live the life I want to live. It is not easy or perfect but it is really living. If I want my life to be better, I will take action and start to make it better. It is not up to someone else, it is up to me. No excuses.

There are 24 hours in a day. If you work for 8 hours and sleep for 8 hours, you still have 8 more hours every day. How are you using that time? Are you wasting it in a long commute? Watching 3 hours of TV? Living vicariously through others on social networks? Trying to recover from a job that is sucking all the energy out of you? There is more to life than that.

It doesn't have to be about drastic measures either. It can be about finally cleaning out the clutter in your life. It is action that brings you joy. It is about creating a new way of life – with small, little steps. It is about *not* being lazy. You need to relax, rejuvenate and take time for yourself and others – but don't be lazy with your *life*.

You need to take responsibility for your life. You need to take action. It is about choosing joy. And it is entirely up to you. I am an *Action Hero* for my life. You are too. You have the power. Now it's up to you.

I am practicing what I preach. I know it's hard. But don't give up before you start. It will be so worth it. You can do this. You can create YOUR *Year of Action* – and I can help. I am so happy and grateful for this *Year of Action!* It is not easy, but I am living *my* BIG, fabulous life. I am choosing joy. I am *living* my life. You can too. It's up to you.

When someone asks you how you spent your one wild and precious life, what will you say?

The journey continues. Come join the *After Party* at: **YearofAction.com**

Acknowledgements

There are so many people who helped to make this book happen:

To those mentioned directly or indirectly in this book, thank you for playing an important part of my life: Heather, Bill and Henry Floyd, Rob McHugh, Rick Schnur, Bob Jacoby, Andy Sugg, Lisa Barnes, Stephanie Bartner, Lily Henderson, Seth Godin, Linda Johnson, The Trademarks, Tasha Irving, Rick Jablonski, Peter Gair, Thierry Delmas, Sharon Whiteley, Thomas White, Diane Hessan, Ben Zander, Susan Stautberg, Edie Weiner, Sheila Shechtman, Rachel Shechtman, Elaine Eisenman, Patti Greene, Cheryl Kiser, Mary Rose, Elizabeth Thornton, Candy Brush, Marlene Casciano, Kristen Palson, Patrician McCarthy, Rita Foley, Janine Craane, Polly Pearson, Camille Preston, Paige Arnof-Fenn, Lara Metcalf, Melissa Means, Sarah Murphy, Sasha Simone, Alison McCrone & Rob Baum, Brandie & Tom Erb, Elliot Offner, Linda Kaplan Thaler, Anne Russo, Laura Furber, Darion Harris, Andrew Deluca, Ashcrofts, Pope & Chris Baratta, Behrents, Biggins, Carberrys, Conroys, Crowleys, Gonçalves, Greenes, Hales, Harnetts, Morisseaus, Phungs, Piersiaks, Sages, The Loud Family, The Marist Girls, The Bridge Club, The Pearls, The Smithies, The TARAs, The Grovers and all my fabulous friends in Worcester and in Medfield.

To Monica Bushnell, Bonnie Newton and Wendy Wirsig, who listened and believed me up in Vermont when I said I was going to change my life – and held me accountable.

To Joanne Gordon, who sat with me on the rocks at *The Brown Owl* and listened and helped me to give myself permission to live my life.

To Diane Maldonado Licalzi and Kathie Devonis Thonis who read the beginnings of the first chapter (while "The Smithies" were all together for one of Nancy and Barry Horowitz's incredible Bat Mitzvah extravaganzas) and urged me to keep writing.

To Diane K. Danielson, who is a brilliant editor, writer, lawyer, social media guru and fashionista – to name a few – who selflessly jumped in to help edit this book and whip it into shape!

Speaking of 'whipping things into shape': To the women at the Medfield *Get in Shape For Women*, Penny Hoodlet, Sybil Kaplan and Linda Wakefield who read first drafts and my trainers Kim Connell, Nancy Johnson, Maria Capobianco, Laura Ingalls along with Liz, Delaney, Andrea, Amy, Sarah & Kelly all of whom are helping me take action to get in shape and transform my body (and life).

To my incredible family who've always been there for me. To Peggy McCormick, Patty Harnett and Nancy McCormick who believed in the book and the blog, from the beginning. To Kate McCormick who read my first chapter out loud and made it seem like it was actually going to become a book. To Kelley McCormick for always being there whenever we need you. To my brother Jim Moran (and family Patty, Mickey, Kyle & Ryan) who has been my coach especially through the tough times, inspires me and shows us all how to have fun in life. To my brother Mike Moran (and family Nancy, Tim & Christina) and Gee Giannino, who call me and make sure I am not starving. To my fabulous sister Maura Moran Cutting (and family Bill, Elizabeth, Joe & Mary) who lived so much of this adventure with me and is always there for me. To my in-laws, Jackie and Bob *(the RAM)* McCormick, who raised a wonderful family and welcomed me in with open arms. To my grandparents Lillian and James Moran and Elizabeth and James Walsh, who dedicated their lives to their families and set such positive examples for all of us. To all the Morans, who laugh often and live a life of giving to others. To Gail Walsh who inspired me to get in shape and to all the Walshes who dream big, live life and support family.

To my mother Mary Moran, the rock of the family, who is a great role model, says "yes" as much as possible and fills our lives with music and laughter. To my dad, the amazing Mickey Moran, who I know is watching over us and helping us in ways I can't even imagine.

To my incredible kids Jack and Lily McCormick, the joys of my life and who put up with my "being in the creative zone" and staring into a computer for long hours to make this book happen. I especially thank my wonderful husband Matt for being my partner and for always supporting me in all my scary, crazy decisions. He was a real force in making this book happen. When I left my job and was finding such joy in writing and I said to him that all I really wanted to do was write, he said, "So do it." So I did.

Thank you all for being part of my one wild and precious life. I am so blessed to have you in it.

ೞ

I look forward to hearing about how you are taking action to stop waiting and start living YOUR big, fabulous life. *Year of Action!*

Come join the *After Party* at: YearofAction.com

Photo Credits

Except where noted, all photos and illustrations courtesy of
Erin Moran McCormick.

Notepad/pencil icon with *Action Steps* – Garsya/Shutterstock.com

13 – Crobard/Shutterstock.com

45 – Dmitri Ometsinsky/Shutterstock.com

46 – By David Gaya (Own work) [GFDL (www.gnu.org/copyleft/fdl.html) or CC-BY-SA-3.0 (www.creativecommons.org/licenses/by-sa/3.0/)], via Wikimedia Commons

48 – By Stanislav Traykov [GFDL (www.gnu.org/copyleft/fdl.html), CC-BY-SA-3.0 (www.creativecommons.org/licenses/by-sa/3.0/) via Wikimedia Commons

52 – Fedyaeva Maria/Shutterstock.com

63– Correggio [Public domain], via Wikimedia Commons

128 – ilolab/Shutterstock.com

139 – Women's Group in Belize: From L to R: Joanne Gordon, Joy Booker, Judithe Registre and Erin McCormick

155 – luxorphoto/Shutterstock.com

166 – Efired/Shutterstock.com

190 – IKO/Shutterstock.com

Bibliography

[1] Godin, Seth. *Linchpin – Are You Indispensable?* (New York: Do You Zoom, Inc., 2010).

[2] Lindberg, Anne Morrow. *The Journey not the Arrival.* (New York: Harcourt, Brace, and World, 1978).

[3] Fairbanks, Amana M. "They Don't Negotiate: Why Young Women College Graduates Are Still Paid Less Than Men", *The Huffington Post,* August 3, 2011.

[4] National Partnership for Women & Families http://blog.nationalpartnership.org/index.php/2011/04.

[5] Babcock, Linda and Sara Laschever. *Ask for it: How Women Can Use the Power of Negotiation to Get What They Really Want* (New York: Bantam 2008).

[6] Huddleston, Peggy. *Prepare for Surgery, Heal Faster. A Guide of Mind-Body Techniques* (Denver: Angel River Press 1996).

[7] Thaler, Linda Kaplan and Robin Koval. *The Power of Nice – How to Conquer the Business World with Kindness* (New York: Crown, 2006).

[8] Seligman, Martin, M.E.P. & Maier, S.F. (1967). Failure to escape traumatic shock. *Journal of Experimental Psychology,* 74, 1–9.

[9] Zander, Ben & Rosamund Stone Zander. *The Art of Possibility: Transforming Professional & Personal Life* (New York: Penguin, 2002).

[10] McCarthy, Patrician. *The Face Reader, Discover Anyone's Personality Through the Chinese Art of Mien Shiang.* (New York: Plume, 2008).

[11] Fresh Air Fund – Freshair.org

[12] Byrne, Rhonda, *The Secret* (New York: Atria Books/Beyond Words 2006).

[13] Foley, Rita and Catherine Allen, Nancy Bearg, Jaye Smith. *Reboot Your Life: Energize Your Career and Life by Taking a Break.* (New York: Beaufort Books, 2011).

[14] Flylady.net

[15] Pinola, Melanie. "Why You Learn More Effectively by Writing Than Typing" *Lifehacker,* January 21, 2011 (http://lifehacker.com/5738093/why-you-learn-more-effectively-by-writing-than-typing)

[16] Ziglar, Zig. http://motivational-stories-fmq.blogspot.com/2007/09/day-before-you-go-on-vacation-by-zig.html

[17] Godin, Seth. Seth's Blog (http://sethgodin.typepad.com)

[18] Kotz, Deborah. "Goal-Oriented: Research Indicates that Willpower can be Strengthened like a muscle-and is a Key Predictor of Success in Life" *Boston Globe,* November 7, 2011.

[19] Gordon, Joanne. *Be Happy at Work: 100 Women Who Love Their Work and Why* (New York: Ballantine Books, 2005).

[20] Ware, Bronnie. *The Top Five Regrets of the Dying* (Bloomington: Balboa Press, 2011).

About the Author

Erin Moran McCormick is an entrepreneur, innovation change agent and award-winning designer. She has spent her career turning ideas into action. McCormick founded three companies: *DAPAH Software*, an online drug prevention curriculum; *Henry's Hearts*, a non-profit gift company; and her newest venture, *Year of Action U*, an online grad school to help women take action and get results in business and life. She earned her degree in art and psychology from Smith College and has been a Creative Director, Executive Producer, CIO and CEO in technology, publishing and education. At age 25 she quit her job, bought a one-way ticket to Europe and started living her *Year of Action*. In the fall of 2011, the 25th anniversary of her *Year of Action*, and her 50th birthday, she quit her job to live her second *Year of Action*. She lives in Medfield, MA with her husband and two children.

ઝ

If I may be so bold…I have a favor to ask. If you like this book and the *Year of Action* way of living, would you help me to spread the word? I would greatly appreciate it if you would stop by **Amazon.com** and leave your comments. Plus, I'd LOVE to hear what you think. Thank you. *Year of Action!*

"Fear not that thy life shall come to an end,

but rather that it shall never have a beginning."

- John Henry Cardinal Newman

ଓଃ

Here's to you beginning to take a step
to stop waiting & start living
your BIG, fabulous life!

Year of Action!

www.YearofAction.com